Wave Maker

Jeff Fisher

Dedication

This book is dedicated to my parents, Kathleen Polise and Ralph Polise. It is a testament to their unwavering love, support, and belief in me. For the countless sacrifices they've made and the endless wisdom they've shared. To my Mother, for her boundless love and nurturing care, and to my Father, who I know is looking down on us, for his endless patience and invaluable teachings. Their strength and resilience have been my guiding stars in every storm.

Acknowledgment

The book that I have created would not have been possible without the help and support of several individuals.

First and foremost, I would like to express my gratitude to my wife, Kristin Fisher, whose unwavering belief in me has been a constant source of inspiration.

I am also deeply thankful to Darryl Zilinskis, whose personal story of resilience and the profound impact of a single act of kindness served as the initial spark for this book.

To my dear friends and family - Alex Hayes, Mark Hansen, Marc Robinson, Bill Fisher, Hasan Ali, Mike Ries, Javon Blue, Donna Cardella, Lucile Polise, Shawn McManus, and Ray Maurone - I offer my heartfelt thanks. Your contributions, both tangible and intangible, have made this work what it is today. I am truly honored and humbled to have your support behind me.

About the Author

The author of this book, Jeff Fisher, is the Founder and Executive Director of the Ride The Wave Foundation. (www.ridethewave.org)

In 1986, when Jeff was four years old, his family moved to Parsippany, NJ. He lived with his mother, brother, and stepfather, Ralph. Growing up, Jeff spent a lot of time outdoors, riding his bike around town and enjoying the company of his friends. Being close to Morristown, New Jersey, provided him with access to a bustling nightlife scene and alternative highways. Moreover, the proximity to both the beach and snowboarding destinations made his hometown an ideal place to grow up.

Jeff did not take the traditional path of graduating high school and going to college. He wasn't the type of student who focused on academics; instead, his attention was drawn to the social aspects of school life. As a result, he acquired valuable social intelligence, which would later prove to be instrumental in his personal development and networking abilities. It wasn't until later in life that Jeff discovered his true strengths and talents, a realization that came hand-in-hand with a diagnosis of bipolar disorder.

The diagnosis of bipolar disorder came as a late revelation, occurring roughly six years ago. Jeff experienced manic episodes and struggled with the associated challenges, leading to hospitalizations and a significant impact on his life. However, he was determined to take control of his condition. Through a combination of daily medication, a morning routine, a carefully managed diet, and a commitment to physical fitness and self-

care, Jeff found ways to mitigate the effects of his disorder. Therapy sessions every other week, both individual and couples therapy, also played a crucial role in his journey toward stability.

After graduating from high school, Jeff didn't immediately pursue college. Instead, he spent time with friends, partying, and working various retail jobs locally. Eventually, he found employment at Cingular Wireless, a cell phone company that later merged with AT&T.

During his time at Cingular Wireless, a chance encounter changed his career path. A customer to whom Jeff sold a BlackBerry was impressed by his sales skills and gave him a business card. The man worked for a staffing agency, and this connection led Jeff to Century Staffing. With their assistance, he tailored his resume and landed several job interviews. Although those interviews didn't result in job offers, Jeff remained persistent.

His perseverance paid off when he secured a position at Vitaquest International, marking his entry into the corporate world. At Vitaquest, he had the guidance of a mentor named Mark Stanisi. Determined to pursue a career in corporate sales, Jeff made the decision to pursue further education. He realized that his parents would no longer be financially supporting his education and took responsibility for his own academic journey. He enrolled in college and earned a degree in project management.

In his mid-20s, armed with his new qualifications, Jeff embarked on his career with newfound motivation. This experience in the business world eventually inspired him to purchase and grow his own company. While his entrepreneurial journey differed from his upbringing, Jeff fondly reminisced about the time he spent engaging in outdoor activities during his childhood. He and his brother would play snow football in their backyard and build snow forts during the winter.

Despite any personal challenges, Jeff enjoyed a comfortable upbringing as his family was relatively well-off. His hometown of Parsippany, New Jersey, provided him with a supportive community and access to various opportunities that shaped his journey into adulthood.

Jeff's post-high school years were marked gain by a departure from the traditional path. While his friends pursued higher education, he chose to remain in his hometown, driven by a desire for a vibrant social life. He immersed himself in the party scene, experimenting with drugs and exploring the club scene in New York City.

This turning point in Jeff's life occurred in his mid-twenties. The partying and experimentation served as a learning experience, fostering his social intelligence and networking skills. Through various jobs and interactions, he honed his ability to build connections and establish a strong network. As time went on, Jeff directed his focus toward developing his leadership abilities, embracing concepts such as servant leadership and positive leadership. His commitment to growth in this area was exemplified by obtaining a leadership certificate from Cornell University.

Once Jeff discovered the direction he wanted to pursue, he became fully invested and began moving forward in his life.

Undoubtedly, there was a critical juncture where he came to a crossroads, aware that he could have easily chosen the wrong path. He experienced minor misdemeanors and witnessed his friends getting into trouble, which gradually diminished the enjoyment he found in his lifestyle.

Reflecting on his unconventional youth, Jeff recognized that his experiences played a pivotal role in shaping his character and personal growth. His journey, marked by challenges and self-discovery, led him to a deeper understanding of himself and the importance of perseverance in overcoming obstacles.

However, Jeff was fortunate to avoid the perils of addiction and substance abuse, a stroke of luck that he couldn't necessarily explain.

While Jeff's behavior in his earlier years may have strayed from the right path, it never reached the point of self-destruction. Rather, it was characterized by a desire for fun experiences under the influence of various substances. Although he came close to going down a more dangerous route, Jeff recognized the potential consequences and made a conscious decision to change course. He vividly recalls a night spent on his parents' deck, contemplating his choices and ultimately choosing a different path.

However, Jeff's decision to veer away from the wrong path did not lead him to develop a sense of pride or superiority over those who had taken different routes in life. He did not look down upon them or carry a chip on his shoulder. Instead, he approached them with empathy and understanding.

Despite having a decent number of friends and a social network during his younger years, Jeff battled with insecurities and a preoccupation with others' opinions. He struggled to maintain eye contact and often worried about what people thought of him. However, over time, he experienced a remarkable transformation. Jeff became a skilled public speaker in his business endeavors, reflecting his newfound confidence and success. This evolution underscored the importance of personal growth and the realization that one's journey is a continuous process toward self-improvement.

Over time, Jeff's insecurities and concerns about others' opinions diminished. He developed into a confident public speaker, finding success in his business endeavors.

Contents

Chapter 1: The Man In The Van

It was a warm summer afternoon. Eli pulled up outside his mother's house in the suburban neighborhood he grew up in. Lots of trees lined the quiet streets, their leaves rustling softly in the breeze.

"Hi, Mom, I'm here!" Eli called as he walked through the door. The familiar smells of home cooking wafted from the kitchen.

His mother emerged, wiping her hands on a dish towel. "Eli, so nice to see you, honey. How have you been?" They embraced.

"I've been good. Just needed a break from the office." Eli stretched his tired muscles. "What's for dinner?"

"Pot roast in the oven. It'll be ready soon." She smiled.

Eli wandered into the kitchen. " I'm parched," declared Eli as he opened the fridge doors with hope.

But all he saw were condiments and leftovers from past meals. He sighed in disappointment. "Nothing here, I'm afraid."

"I guess I used the last of the OJ this morning," his mom replied apologetically.

"I guess I'll have to make a trip to the convenience store," said Eli as he grabbed the keys.

"Be back in a bit," he said as he locked the front door behind him and began the short walk down the street.

It was a pleasant afternoon - the sun shone warmly, and a light breeze rustled the tree leaves.

As he passed the corner, his eyes wandered as they often did. That's when he noticed the old blue van parked under a large oak tree. It looked like it had seen better days - tape was holding part of the bumper, and rust spots dotted the sides.

Eli glanced in the window as he walked by out of curiosity. That's when he saw the man reclined in the front seat, eyes closed in slumber. Even from outside, Eli could see the signs of weariness on his face.

He continued to the store, the cool air washing over him as he entered. After perusing the selections, Eli grabbed the OJ. He paid and started back the way he came.

As Eli paused by the van, he felt something come over him. A soft wave of warmth and love. Why did he feel compelled to stop and check on the man in the van? He was nervous to approach, but he decided to respond. Curiosity got the best of him, and he tapped lightly on the window.

"Excuse me, sir?" Eli called out softly.

The man inside jumped with a start, clearly not expecting to be woken. Their eyes met through the glass.

"Sorry, I didn't mean to scare you. Are you alright?" Eli asked with concern.

The man blinked sleep from his eyes. "Uh, yeah, I'm fine. Why do you ask?"

Eli gestured to the van. "I've noticed you parking here often. Just wanted to make sure everything's okay."

The man hesitated, then replied, "I'm Darryl. Yeah, been sleeping in my van for a while now." His face showed the exhaustion of his situation.

Sensing Darryl's reluctance to share more, Eli spoke gently. "It's okay, you don't have to say. But if there's any way I can help..."

Darryl gazed at him, guarded. Then, his defenses seemed to crack. "Truth is, I've fallen on hard times. Lost my job and home."

His voice shook with emotion held in too long. Eli listened attentively, empathizing silently.

"Things will get better," Eli reassured. "Wait here. I'll be right back." He hurried off to the store, mind racing on how to lift Darryl's spirits.

Inside the convenience store, Eli took a moment to think. How could he best help Darryl in his current desperate situation? While Eli didn't like directly handing out money, he again responded to a feeling and decided this was the best course of action.

Some cash would allow Darryl shelter, a warm meal, and a chance to pull himself back up. His mind was made up, and Eli marched to the ATM with purpose. He silently withdrew what he thought was enough, which was more than he typically felt comfortable with. But Darryl's plight had moved him deeply.

Returning to the van, Eli pushed through his nerves again. What if Darryl refused the gift, thinking him insincere? As he rapped gently on the window, Eli hoped his empathy had shone through.

The glass slid open slowly. "I'm back," Eli said gently. Without a word, he held out the cash bundled in his hand.

Darryl stared at the bundled cash in disbelief. His weathered hands shook as he slowly reached to accept the gift. "I... I don't know what to say," he stammered.

"You don't need to say anything. Just take it and get yourself back on your feet," Eli replied with a smile.

Nodding numbly, Darryl carefully tucked the money away.

"I'll leave you be now. But you take care, alright?" With a final nod, Eli turned to go.

As the van door slid shut, isolating Darryl once more within its walls, the dam finally broke. Tears flowed unrestrained down his gaunt cheeks.

Such kindness from a stranger was more than he could have ever dreamed of receiving in his lowest hour. The encounter had ignited a small flame of hope in Darryl's weary heart. For the first time in months, a sense of purpose stirred in the shadows of his despair.

That impactful interaction really stuck with Eli. Seeing how much the small act of kindness meant to Darryl in his time of need gave Eli a new perspective on the importance of community support. Now, he tried to give back whenever possible, whether through regular donations or volunteering his time.

Eli also found himself more observant of those around him who appeared to be struggling. If he noticed someone like Darryl had been down on their luck with nowhere to turn, he made it a point to check in. He learned that a simple "Hey, just wanted to make sure you have what you need" could go a long way. You never knew what difference a small gesture might make.

Reaching out to Darryl that day opened Eli's eyes to a new way of living. He embraced paying kindness forward and looking out for others in his neighborhood, a priority he hadn't focused on before. Eli believed people must band together and support one another, especially in these uncertain times. Even the smallest act of care or compassion could lift someone from their lowest point. He was glad he took the chance that day, as it taught him an important lesson—one he always carried with him.

Months had passed since Eli's chance encounter with Darryl. One Sunday afternoon, Eli was driving through the neighborhood with his fiancée Kristin. She knew the story of how Eli had helped Darryl, which had profoundly shaped Eli's outlook.

They were preparing to attend the Entre Leadership Conference in Nashville the following week. While it wasn't a vacation, Eli looked forward to spending quality time with Kristin in the city.

As they drove by the familiar street corner, Eli felt the wave come over him again. He continued to ride the wave once again with no fear this time. He swung the car back around. "I just want to check something," he told Kristin.

When they pulled up, Eli saw the old blue van parked in its usual spot. And glancing in, he was surprised to see Darryl sitting in the front seat - but this time, he had a passenger.

Eli rolled down the window and called out. Darryl glanced over in recognition, his face breaking into a grin. Eli was stunned by the change - Darryl's shoulders looked broader, his eyes vibrant and full of life. Gone was the gaunt exhaustion that had clung to him before.

Catching up briefly, Darryl told Eli all that had changed since their fateful meeting. Thanks to Eli's help, Darryl was getting his life back on track. Witnessing this transformation firsthand moved Eli deeply and served as a reminder of the impact one act of kindness can make.

As Eli spoke with Darryl, he was overcome with emotion. He was so moved by the incredible change he witnessed in this man who had been at such a low point before.

Saying goodbye, Eli walked back to the car in a daze. He noticed Kristin looking at him with concern. When he got in, the tears started flowing uncontrollably.

Kristin pulled away from the curb as Eli broke down completely. Nothing could hold back the flood of feelings hearing what an impact he'd had on Darryl's life.

They drove down the street until Eli gently asked Kristin to pull over. He stepped out of the car, walking a short distance to the edge of a driveway, where he let the emotions pour out of him unchecked.

Great heaving sobs wracked Eli's body as he wept tears of both joy and sorrow. Seeing Darryl's transformation from that hopeless day they'd met was overwhelming and transformative.

For the rest of the week leading up to the conference, Eli carried that experience with him. An amazing well of energy and inspiration fueled his work and conversations. He couldn't stop thinking about the power one small act of kindness held to change someone's world. It was a moment he'd never forget.

For Eli, that interaction represented a new beginning - a renewed commitment to paying compassion forward however he could. Attending the leadership conference buoyed by the experience, Eli felt compelled to share Darryl's story.

Eli attended a sponsorship breakfast at the conference; he listened intently to Ken Coleman's insightful remarks. Ken is a best-selling author and host of the Ken Coleman Show; he is someone Eli looks up to. When Ken finished speaking and walked alone down the hall, Eli saw his chance. Fighting nerves, he leaped up and hurriedly walked out of the room while everyone else was seated. He introduced himself and praised Ken's work.

When Eli asked if he could share a story, Ken graciously heard him out. Retelling what happened with Darryl, Eli grew emotional once more. He sensed their encounter encompassed a valuable lesson about the power of small kindnesses.

To Eli's relief, Ken listened with empathy and understanding. He encouraged Eli to spread the message of hope to others at the conference. So, Eli shared their story whenever he found a listening ear.

People responded deeply to the tale of humanity and transformation. It resonated in a way that inspired further discussion of ways to lift each other up, especially the vulnerable. Eli left feeling he had sowed an important seed, one that might someday blossom into even greater change.

Ever since that fateful interaction with Darryl, Eli's life underwent many positive changes. Sharing their story at the leadership conference opened new doors. Inspired leaders saw Eli's potential, and he gained valuable skills and connections.

This empowered Eli to revitalize his own company's culture with a renewed focus on empowering employees and uplifting the community. He instilled the valuable lesson of paying kindness forward through outreach initiatives.

The leadership conference opened Eli's eyes to a whole new level of possibilities. By circulating ideas, networking genuinely with others, and interacting behind the scenes, new opportunities emerged.

He realized the most impactful change doesn't always happen publicly through media attention. Real progress unfolds through quiet, meaningful connections between dedicated individuals. Eli was inspired by the vast network of kindhearted people working diligently behind the scenes.

He began seeking such connections more proactively instead of passively receiving surface-level information. If more people tapped into this undercurrent of goodwill, imagine the potential ripple effects.

For Eli, these interactions held a deep meaning that far surpassed any fleeting pleasures of the external world. Being genuine, getting to know others, and lending help without expectation touched his spirit in a pure way.

Each new encounter unveiled a whole life history and perspective he couldn't have known otherwise. People possessed far more depth than superficial judgments allowed. Eli was constantly reminded how small kindnesses could transform lives and bring unlikely people together for the greater good.

Chapter 2: Radiate Positive Energy

Just like a calm sea on a sunny day, approach people with a friendly demeanor, a warm smile, and eye contact to make yourself approachable.

Making a strong first impression is important for forming new relationships. Yet initiating contact with strangers can be intimidating, as fears of awkward silence or saying the wrong thing often hold us back. The secret to overcoming these anxieties and attracting positive attention lies in radiating confidence from within.

Positive energy is a feeling of optimism, warmth, and genuineness that shines through one's entire demeanor. It creates an inviting aura that draws people in and makes them eager to learn more. Rather than something we're born with or artificially project, positive energy stems from believing in ourselves and finding the lightness in each moment.

When we approach others with positive energy, our body language conveys ease. Standing tall with an open posture, making eye contact, and smiling freely shows that we feel comfortable in our own skin. Our tone of voice remains upbeat and engaging.

Positive energy also gives us the courage to steer conversations past any lulls gracefully. Overall, radiating positivity through authentic confidence is the best way to make memorable first impressions and foster new connections. By developing this energy within, fears of rejection disappear, paving the path to meaningful relationships.

Why Be Positive?

While the anxious little voice in your head might warn against optimism in unfamiliar circles, I'm here to tell you - positive vibes are key to working a room! When opportunities arise to mingle, leave your inner Eeyore at home and instead pack your most effervescent energy. Walk in with the wattage dialed to 11 and watch the friendships spark.

See, an upbeat aura has an allure that draws people in like moths to a flame. With confidence radiating from your million-dollar grin and swagger in your stride, you silently signal that you've got nothing to fear and everything fabulous to share.

Leave the mopey vibes to sulk at home - a positive presence is akin to gold in the friendship market. Not only will charmers flock your way, but your good vibes are guaranteed to be contagious.

Just one flash of those pearly whites is all it takes for even the frostiest folks to start cracking smiles. Your warm and welcoming ways quickly thaw anyone holding up a cold exterior.

With positivity raising the mood, genuine chuckles and real conversations can smoothly flow without any awkward pretense.

Plus, a vibrant spirit makes you utterly unforgettable. While others drone on with dull drear, your radiant reactions and funny quips will have every head turning your way. Leave an impression that lasts long after new acquaintances leave. People will be reminiscing about your exuberance long after the fun is done!

And trust, in a caring and curious way, spreads influence like wildfire. Showing empathy and compassion inspires people to bring out their best, brightest selves. When you throw positivity into the mix, it does not take long for bonds to form. Create this feel-good atmosphere and watch relationships blossom at rapid speed.

How to Radiate Positive Energy

Now that you know the benefits of positive energy, how can you radiate it when you approach people? Here are some tips to help you out:

Be yourself: The first step to sharing your light is embracing who you truly are. There's no need to put on false pretenses. When you proudly live in your values and truths, you automatically start to radiate positivity. People feel authenticity intimately and gravitate toward those comfortable in their own skin. Appreciating your talents and areas for growth, your unique passions, and your journey - this intimate self-acceptance is radiant. It inspires others to walk their own paths unapologetically, too. Your genuine spirit uplifts all it touches.

Be positive: The second step to radiate positive energy is to be positive. I know this may seem like a no-brainer, but hear me out. To be positive is to maintain a positive outlook on life, focus on the bright side of things, and express gratitude for what you have. Being positive also means avoiding negative thoughts, words, and actions, such as complaining, criticizing, or gossiping. Negative energy is an instant turnoff for most. It makes people feel uncomfortable or defensive. Positive energy, on the other hand, can attract people and make them feel happy and relaxed.

This means consciously choosing to have a hopeful perspective on life wherever possible. It involves making an effort to look on the bright side of any situation and counting your blessings for what you do have rather than dwelling on what is lacking. Adopting a positive mindset also means limiting negative self-talk and avoiding putting others down through complaints, criticisms, or spreading rumors. A negative thought pattern can gradually bring one's own mood down over time. It can also put people off if you constantly bring up negative ideas in every social setting. In contrast, positive energy has the power to draw people in and make them feel comfortable and content. When you behave and communicate with optimism.

Be friendly: The third step of emanating positive vibes is to treat everyone you encounter with kindness and respect. Being friendly requires making a conscious choice to behave politely, courteously, and inclusively toward others, no matter their social status, background, or outward appearance. It means going out of your way to demonstrate warmth and welcome everyone you meet. Displaying friendly body language, such as making eye contact, smiling, and using an upbeat tone, shows genuine interest and curiosity in people. These friendly behaviors signal that you are approachable and likable. People instinctively feel at ease and are more willing to open up when interacting with those emitting friendly energy. Displaying friendliness encourages connections and builds trust between yourself and others.

Be expressive: The tone, voice, and words we use to communicate with our inner selves are essential to the fourth step of radiating positive energy. Conveying emotions, thoughts, and personality through lively body language, tone of voice, and the words we choose helps spread positivity. Being expressive also allows our spontaneous, creative, and playful side to emerge. Add humor, personal anecdotes, or compliments to interactions to liven them up. Expression is what makes us seem vibrant, engaging, and interesting. It adds spice, color, and energy to conversations that draw people in.

We've covered the importance of positive energy when meeting new people. But no interaction begins until that first moment of contact. How you initiate communications with someone you've never met sets the tone for future interactions. Your energy in those first seconds leaves a lasting impression and determines whether they'll be open to connecting or put on the defensive. It's a crucial phase that can either pave the way for a great conversation or end it before it starts.

In the next chapter, we'll uncover the secrets to captivating even the most unsure stranger from the first meeting. When you turn the page, you'll gain the power to light up any room you enter. For now, keep radiating that positivity.

Chapter 3: Nerves are Normal

Like a turbulent sea, your nerves can toss you adrift. Find solace in the calm depths within. Breathe deeply, let the waves settle, and navigate toward tranquility.

You see someone across the room that catches your eye.

As you gaze at the stranger, your heart pounds like the relentless pounding of the surf against the rugged cliffs. Thoughts swirl like storm clouds in your head.

The sea of anxiety stretches out before you, vast and unpredictable.

Each step closer to the stranger feels like navigating treacherous waters, unsure of the currents that may pull you under. Your palms grow clammy, and your breath becomes shallow.

Clouds of doubt your thinking as all the possible negative outcomes flash through your imagination.

Your palms start to feel sweaty with anticipation. You wipe them casually on your pants, hoping whoever it is hasn't noticed your nerves from all the way over there. Taking a deep breath, you start to psyche yourself. But it's hard to silence the doubts with so much riding on this interaction.

As you take the first steps in their direction, it feels like your feet are stuck in the mud. Each movement brings you closer but also increases your nerves tenfold. You can feel your heart pounding in your chest so hard you're sure they must be able to see it. But there's no backing out now. You're committed to taking the chance.

Let's pause for a second. Where did all this anxiety even come from anyway?

The heightened nervousness, worry, and self-consciousness that arises when initiating social interactions or exposing oneself to potential social situations is called Approach Anxiety.

The biological mechanisms that drive approach anxiety involve the overactivation of the amygdala (the fear center of the brain) and the underactivation of the prefrontal cortex (logic/rational thinking center). This can make irrational worries and physical sensations of anxiety feel very real and hard to control.

Approach anxiety isn't just about meeting new people. It can involve interacting with any unfamiliar person or situation, like public speaking, dating, job interviews, and more. The core fear is being negatively judged or rejected.

These anxieties tend to be most intense during the anticipation phase rather than the interaction itself. Once engagement begins, those uncomfortable feelings often subside quickly.

If you feel like the only one feeling like this, you'll be glad to know you're not in it alone. Approach anxiety is common, affecting up to 20% of the population at some point.

The good news is that with time and sustained effort, approach anxiety is very treatable. Gaining awareness of it can help reduce shame and motivate you to seek effective treatment and begin self-help strategies.

First, you would have to examine the root cause. Why do you feel the way you do?

Perhaps it stems from the teachings you received as a child. You distinctly recall your parents warning you not to talk to strangers, drilling it into your head from a young age as a safety precaution. While well-meaning, this may have unconsciously framed strangers as potential threats rather than neutral acquaintances. It sets a baseline assumption of risk in any interaction with an unfamiliar person.

On a basic biological level, socializing with unfamiliar people triggers threat responses for survival reasons. Millennia of evolution shaped the flight-or-fight nervous system to err on the side of caution when assessing strangers for potential danger.

While helpful ancestral heuristics, this wiring provides little differentiation between genuine risks and mere social awkwardness in today's much safer world.

Maybe it's because you hold yourself at a lower level; individuals with low self-esteem often internalize negative beliefs about themselves, like being boring, unlikable, or not good enough. They perceive interactions as judgments of their worthiness, making rejection feel catastrophic.

This leads us to the fear of rejection. Rejection sensitivity is common, with an intrinsic need for acceptance fueling worrisome "what if" scenarios. The human imagination conjures many scenarios with terrible outcomes.

There might also be something within you that requires every interaction to be the very best. It's either that or no interaction at all.

A single awkward exchange is personalized as a character flaw rather than a common human experience. Perfectionism fuels worries over saying "the right thing" lest they be disqualified from someone's approval altogether.

Putting interactions "on a pedestal" transforms an opportunity for connection into a high-stakes performance with intense scrutiny. Imagination runs wild, envisioning how every little perceived flaw, from word choice to body language, will be harshly ragged on later.

You may perceive a negative reaction and assume "people don't like me" as a universally true statement rather than an isolated experience.

So, as you stand here, a lifetime of potent direct and vicarious conditioning swirls underneath one introduction. It's a testament to courage that you're willing to disrupt those inclinations, however maladaptive, for the sake of one friendly gesture.

Maybe it's not all that we mentioned above. Whatever the reasons might be, the good news is that approach anxiety is not chronic. Here are some ways you can shake off the nerves and approach people confidently.

Reframe Introductions as Low-Stakes: Remind yourself that, chances are, the other person is also focused on their own worries instead of intensely scrutinizing and judging you. Most people are understanding about nervousness. See interactions as opportunities rather than tests where you pass or fail based on their approval. Accept that while wanting inclusion, you cannot control external reactions entirely.

Cast Doubt on Anxious Predictions: Question assumptions like "they won't like me" by considering alternatives - perhaps you share an interest, spark a fun conversation, or they're happy for interaction, too. Hunches are not facts, so experiment to see things unfold better than expected. Remember, there is variability in human nature instead of expecting definitive conclusions from minimal data.

Normalize Nerves: Remind yourself that feeling anxious is part of the shared human experience. Your worth isn't defined by comfort in social situations alone, as opportunities for growth exist in facing challenges respectfully. Be patient with yourself as skills strengthen over time in relaxed practice rather than worrying about perfection from the start. Progress, not arrival, is the goal.

Reframe Rejection: While validation feels good, one person's disinterest does not negate your whole existence or undo moments of ease with others. External perception says more about them. Choose not to internalize fleeting interactions as character judgments but seek your worth from within through virtues like courage, patience, and understanding.

Practice Self-Compassion: Speak to yourself as gently as you would encourage a friend. Counter harsh criticisms with encouragement and understanding of your inherent lovability outside validation from any interaction alone. Develop calm self-acceptance to spread warmth to exchanges naturally. Growth happens through non-judgmental awareness.

Finally, remind yourself that the stranger before you is also a person with their own fears and vulnerabilities. Like you, they may be navigating their own sea of emotions.

You've got this!

Chapter 4: Deliver a Warm Greeting

Start the interaction with a genuine "Hello" or "Hi," like a gentle wave greeting the shore to set a positive tone.

The energy we emit before we engage in contact has a substantial impact on how we will be perceived. But how you engage is equally important.

The moment of first contact is perhaps the most crucial yet underappreciated stage of meeting someone new. Before words are exchanged, within the first few seconds, judgments are already formed. It's so important to be mindful of how your approach comes across because first impressions really do impact the whole interaction, for it is within these fleeting moments that you can build rapport or have walls erected against you.

Start the interaction with a genuine "Hello" or "Hi," like a gentle wave greeting the shore to set a positive tone.

Your goal in extending that first greeting should be simple - to put the other person in comfort while also generating intrigue. You want them to feel relaxed yet curious to continue talking. Striking this balance right away paves the way for easy conversation and a positive impression that lasts long after you've parted ways.

But a warm, confident greeting opens doors by setting both parties at ease right from the start. With so much riding on such a brief window, it is crucial to make it count.

Leading with a genuine "hey" or "what's up" is such an easy way to kick things off on the right note. It's like you're saying, "I'm here and happy to see you!" without being overly formal.

People appreciate when you take that first step to say hi instead of waiting around awkwardly. And keeping it casual but friendly helps them feel relaxed straight off the bat. Trust me; nobody wants to feel like they're being interviewed from Hello!

The key is putting warmth into those simple words through your smile and tone. Make eye contact so they know you really want to connect, even if you're exchanging a quick "what's up" in passing.

It's all about sparking positivity from the start. Just like we talked about before, with radiating positive energy, you really want your greeting to match that upbeat, welcoming vibe. Even if it's something simple like "Hey" or "What's up," put that smile and positivity you've been cultivating into it.

When people feel the genuine warmth and enthusiasm you're bringing, it immediately puts them at ease. They'll mirror that energy, too, which gets the interaction off to a lively start. And we all know more positive connections make the world go round!

So, think of greeting people in a way that reflects how you've been brightly shining your light. Convey through your smile, tone, and body language that you're excited to connect, even just in passing. Holding space for others with care always lifts the mood.

By keeping things light but sincere, you invite them to join you in the optimistic spirit you've been radiating outward. It shows interacting with you is a chance to soak up some of those good vibes, too!

Once you feel confident beaming positivity from within, your "hey" or "hi" will extend that enthusiasm naturally. Just focus on spreading the good energy you cultivate right from the very beginning. Ignite a spark in their day like you do for others - it goes a long way.

A warm greeting provides an immediate benefit to both parties by conveying friendliness and approachability. But its impact extends far beyond those first seconds. Mastering the art of a thoughtful introduction sets the tone for positive engagement long-term in several key ways:

Comfort and Rapport: By using body language and words that communicate care, respect, and interest, you help the other person feel at ease. This relaxed atmosphere allows a genuine rapport to develop organically from the earliest stage. Rather than facing each other as strangers, a comfortable familiarity is established where open discussion can flow.

Trust and Goodwill: A welcoming introduction signals that you come in good faith, with the goal of harmonious interaction rather than conflict or hidden agendas. This fosters an instinctive trust that serves as fertile ground for new acquaintances to truly get to know one another beyond the surface level. Goodwill is the foundation for lasting connections.

Enthusiasm and Investment: A warm greeting conveys enthusiasm for meeting the other person and learning more about them. This conveys your invested presence in the conversation and gives them confidence that engaging with you will be a positive experience. People naturally gravitate toward others, radiating lively positivity and interest.

Smooth Continuation: Starting off on the right relaxed note maintains a pleasant trajectory instead of risking awkward lulls or stilted back-and-forth interactions. Participants feel motivated to keep the discussion flowing smoothly and naturally. This continuity allows for a deeper conversation that expands understanding on both sides.

Emotional Uplift: A sincere, friendly welcome leaves the other person feeling seen, acknowledged, and valued from the very beginning. This has a profound emotional impact that encourages openness on an intuitive level. Relating on an uplifting note primes both individuals to gain optimism from the social exchange.

Memorability: A positive first impression rooted in warmth creates a vivid, lasting memory of the encounter. This makes you more likely to be perceived favorably going forward and potentially reconnect again if opportunities arise. Leaving such an imprint has an advantage in both personal and professional domains.

Most people would likely agree that giving a warm greeting is fairly straightforward. After all, a simple "hello" with a smile seems like a pretty basic social skill.

However, there are actually some nuanced factors that don't necessarily occur naturally to everyone. While a friendly greeting may seem like a no-brainer, there are some subtle elements involved that people may not always be aware of.

One of the biggest is coming on too strong right off the bat. While radiating positivity is great, take care not to conflate it with being overeager or intrusive, lest you risk crossing boundaries and making others uncomfortable.

Failing to read the room or body language is another way you shoot yourself in the foot when engaging other people. If they seem shy or distracted, don't try to force a conversation. Pushing too hard when they're not ready or interested can damage their initial perception of you. Pay attention to subtle verbal and nonverbal cues, so you know when to step back versus connect more.

Then there's coming across as disengaged or distracted. Maybe you're on your phone as they approach or glance around uninterested. That projects aloofness rather than a warm presence. Make solid eye contact, smile, and give them your undivided focus to seem invested from hello.

Man, who would have thought something as simple as a greeting could have so many layers to it? When we started digging into this chapter, I'll admit I was like, "How hard can it be to say hi?" But wow, there's definitely more to it than meets the eye.

We do so many little things without even realizing it - like making eye contact, smiling with feeling, matching someone's energy. And don't even get me started on reading the room and adapting your approach based on the vibes. You've probably never stopped to think about tuning into all those non-verbal cues before.

Now I get that it takes practice to nail all the finer points. It's one thing to learn about it and another to actually apply it smoothly at the moment. But I tell you, just having this framework in my back pocket will make you feel way more confident starting conversations.

For sure, keeping things flowing after the intro is the real test. But at least we've got a solid starting point now. Anyway, let me stop rambling. Let's move on to the next chapter, which explores what to do after the first hello.

Chapter 5: Be Genuine and Authentic

Like the vast and ever-changing ocean, our true selves run deep. When we approach others with genuine openness, we invite them into the tranquil shallows of our authentic spirit, creating an immediate sense of trust. Authenticity is the lighthouse that guides us through the fog of self-doubt, giving us the courage to let our unique light shine, unafraid of judgment. Just as the ocean's salty spray nourishes the coastline, our genuine self has the power to enrich the lives of those we encounter. So cast off the constraints of pretense and let your authentic nature emerge, for in embracing who you truly are, you open the door to meaningful, lasting connections - the kind that run as deep as the boundless sea.

The ballroom of the Grand Plaza Hotel buzzed with the chatter of hundreds of professionals, all dressed in their finest attire. Chandeliers cast a warm glow over the crowd, their light glinting off champagne flutes and polished name badges. Emma stood at the edge of the room, a glass of white wine in her hand, observing the scene before her with a mixture of curiosity and unease.

As the company's annual networking gala unfolded around her, Emma couldn't shake the feeling that something was off. She watched as her colleague, Mark, laughed a little too loudly at their CEO's joke, his eyes darting around the room as if to ensure others had noticed his show of camaraderie. Nearby, Sarah from accounting was deep in conversation with a potential client, her smile plastered on so firmly it looked painful.

Emma sipped her wine, her brow furrowing as she continued to scan the room. Everywhere she looked, she saw the same thing: people going through the motions, saying the right words, laughing at the right moments, but somehow missing the mark of genuine interaction.

She thought back to the family reunion she'd attended just last weekend. The same sense of disconnect had pervaded that gathering, too. Aunt Linda had asked about Emma's job, but her eyes had already moved on to the next relative before Emma could finish answering. Uncle Bob had regaled the family with the same fishing story he told every year, while cousins nodded politely, their attention clearly elsewhere.

As the evening wore on, Emma found herself retreating further into her own thoughts. She realized that what she was witnessing wasn't unique to this event or even to her family gathering. It was a pattern, a societal norm that had become so ingrained that most people didn't even notice it anymore.

People were hiding behind carefully constructed personas, presenting the version of themselves they thought others wanted to see. They were actors on a stage, playing the roles they believed were expected of them. Emma felt a pang of empathy as she recognized her own tendency to do the same.

How many times had she nodded along in meetings, afraid to voice her true opinions? How often had she given a polite "I'm fine" when asked how she was, even on days when she was struggling? She was just as guilty of perpetuating this cycle of inauthenticity as anyone else in the room.

s this realization washed over her, Emma felt a sudden urge to break free from the pattern. She was tired of the superficial interactions and constant performance. She yearned for something real, something genuine.

Taking a deep breath, Emma made a decision. Her next conversation would be different. She would drop the act, let down her guard, and allow herself to be truly seen. The thought both terrified and exhilarated her.

Emma scanned the room, looking for an opportunity. Her eyes landed on a man standing alone near the buffet table, looking as out of place as she felt. She didn't recognize him, which meant he was likely from one of the company's other branches or perhaps a guest of another employee.

Setting down her wine glass, Emma squared her shoulders and made her way across the room. As she approached, the man looked up, a flicker of surprise crossing his face.

"Hi," Emma said, extending her hand. "I'm Emma. I don't think we've met before."

The man shook her hand, a polite smile forming on his lips. "Nice to meet you, Emma. I'm David. I'm here with my wife. She works in the marketing department."

Emma nodded, feeling the familiar pull to fall into the usual small talk routine. But she resisted, reminding herself of her resolution to be authentic.

"You know, David," she said, her heart pounding, "I have a confession to make. I've spent the last hour watching everyone at this party, including myself, put on these perfect, polished personas. And I'm exhausted by it. So I'm going to try something different. Instead of asking what you do for a living or how you're enjoying the party, I'm going to tell you that I'm feeling overwhelmed and a little bit lonely in this crowd of people. And I'd really like to have a genuine conversation with someone if you're up for it."

David's eyes widened, clearly taken aback by Emma's candor. For a moment, she feared she'd made a terrible mistake. But then, something in his expression shifted. The polite mask he'd been wearing seemed to melt away, replaced by a look of relief and curiosity.

"Wow," he said, letting out a soft chuckle. "I wasn't expecting that. But you know what? I feel exactly the same way. I've been standing here for the past twenty minutes, trying to work up the courage to talk to someone, anyone, without sounding like a rehearsed LinkedIn profile."

Emma felt a wave of relief wash over her. "It's exhausting, isn't it? Always trying to present the perfect image of ourselves?"

David nodded enthusiastically. "Absolutely. I mean, don't get me wrong, I love my wife, and I'm happy to support her at these events. But I always feel like such an outsider. Like everyone else has the script for how to act, and I'm the only one improvising."

As they continued to talk, Emma was amazed at how quickly the conversation deepened. They shared stories about their struggles with social anxiety, laughed about their most awkward networking attempts, and even delved into their hopes and fears for the future.

At one point, David confessed, "You know, I've always dreamed of opening my own bakery. But I've never told anyone except my wife. It seems so frivolous compared to what everyone else is doing with their lives."

Emma felt a surge of warmth towards this man she'd just met. "That doesn't sound frivolous at all," she said earnestly. "It sounds brave. To pursue something you're passionate about, regardless of what others might think? That's admirable."

As their conversation wound down, David looked at Emma with genuine gratitude. "I can't tell you how refreshing this has been," he said. "Your willingness to be vulnerable from the get-go made me feel like it was okay to be myself, too. Thank you for that."

Emma felt a lump form in her throat. "Thank you for being receptive to it," she replied. "I wasn't sure how this would go, but I'm so glad I took the chance."

As she made her way home that night, Emma couldn't stop thinking about her interaction with David. The stark contrast between that genuine exchange and the countless superficial conversations she'd observed (and participated in) earlier in the evening was striking.

She thought about how quickly she and David had formed a connection, how seen and understood she had felt in those moments. It was as if, by dropping their masks, they had created a small oasis of authenticity in a desert of pretense.

Emma realized that this approach to interaction – leading with vulnerability and authenticity – had the power to transform not just individual conversations but potentially her entire approach to relationships.

She thought about her job, where she often felt pressured to project constant confidence and competence, even when she was struggling or unsure. What if she allowed herself to admit when she needed help or didn't have all the answers? How might that change the dynamic with her colleagues?

She considered her family relationships, often characterized by polite distance and avoidance of difficult topics. What if she initiated more honest conversations about her feelings, her fears, and her hopes? Could it lead to deeper, more meaningful connections with her loved ones?

As she pondered these possibilities, Emma felt a mix of excitement and trepidation. Being authentic, she realized, wasn't always easy. It required courage, a willingness to be vulnerable, and the ability to sit with discomfort. There was always the risk of rejection or misunderstanding.

But the potential rewards – genuine connections, deeper relationships, a sense of being truly known and accepted – seemed worth the risk.

As she prepared for bed that night, Emma made a decision. She would commit to being more mindful of her own tendencies to wear a mask and present a curated version of herself to the world. And she would make a conscious effort to remove that mask more often, to embrace and share her true self.

She knew it wouldn't be easy. Years of societal conditioning and personal habits wouldn't disappear overnight. There would be times when she'd fall back into old patterns, times when the vulnerability felt too scary or the potential for judgment too high.

However, she also knew that the experience with David had given her a glimpse of what was possible when people allowed themselves to be authentic. And that glimpse was too powerful, too transformative to ignore.

As she drifted off to sleep, Emma felt a sense of purpose and excitement she hadn't experienced in years. Tomorrow would be the first day of her journey towards greater authenticity. She didn't know exactly where this path would lead her, but she was eager to find out.

The next morning, as Emma prepared for work, she stood in front of her mirror, taking in her reflection. She saw the same face she'd seen countless times before, but somehow, it looked different today. There was a spark in her eyes, a subtle shift in her expression that spoke of newfound determination.

As she applied her makeup, Emma made a conscious decision to keep it minimal. Usually, she'd put on a full face, armor against the world's scrutiny. Today, she opted for just a touch of mascara and lip balm. It was a small act of authenticity, allowing her natural self to shine through.

On her commute to work, Emma found herself more aware of her surroundings and the people in them. She noticed a young man nervously adjusting his tie, likely headed to a job interview. Instead of averting her eyes as she normally would, Emma caught his gaze and offered a reassuring smile. The man's shoulders visibly relaxed, and he smiled back gratefully.

Arriving at her office, Emma took a deep breath before stepping out of the elevator. The marketing firm where she worked was known for its competitive atmosphere, and she'd always felt the need to project an image of unwavering confidence and competence.

As she walked to her desk, her colleague Sarah called out, "Morning, Emma! How did the networking event go last night?"

Emma paused, considering her response. Normally, she'd offer a generic "It was great, thanks!" and move on. But today, she decided to be more honest.

"You know what, Sarah? It was a bit overwhelming, to be honest. But I ended up having a really meaningful conversation with someone, which made the whole evening worthwhile."

Sarah looked surprised for a moment, then her expression softened. "I know what you mean," she confided. "Those events can be so draining. I'm glad you found a bright spot."

This small exchange left Emma feeling lighter. She realized that by being more genuine, she'd opened the door for Sarah to do the same.

As the day progressed, Emma found more opportunities to practice authenticity. In a team meeting, when her boss asked for input on a new project, Emma admitted that she had concerns about the timeline instead of simply nodding along with everyone else. To her surprise, several colleagues agreed, leading to a productive discussion about realistic goals and resource allocation.

During lunch, instead of eating at her desk while scrolling through emails, Emma invited a new intern to join her in the break room. She asked the young woman about her aspirations and shared some of her own early career struggles, creating a bond that went beyond the usual mentor-mentee dynamic.

By the end of the workday, Emma felt both exhilarated and exhausted. Being authentic required more energy and courage than she'd anticipated. There had been moments of discomfort, like when she'd had to disagree with a senior colleague's suggestion politely. But overall, she felt more connected to her coworkers and more satisfied with her interactions than she had in months.

As she packed up her things, Emma's phone buzzed with a text from her mother: "Don't forget, family dinner tonight at 7!"

Emma felt a flutter of anxiety in her stomach. Family dinners were often a breeding ground for the kind of superficial interactions she was trying to avoid. However, she also recognized it as an opportunity to extend her authenticity experiment into her personal life.

Arriving at her parents' house, Emma was greeted by the familiar chorus of "How are you?" and "You look great!"s. Instead of falling into the usual pattern of polite but distant conversation, Emma took a deep breath and decided to be more open.

When her aunt asked how work was going, instead of the standard "It's going well," Emma shared her excitement about a challenging project she was working on, as well as her fears about meeting the high expectations placed on her. Her aunt listened intently, then surprised Emma by sharing her own experiences of workplace pressure from her days as a young lawyer.

During dinner, when the conversation turned to her cousin's recent engagement, Emma found the courage to express her own mixed feelings about relationships and marriage. Instead of the judgment she feared, she was met with understanding and even relief from family members who admitted to having similar doubts and fears.

As the evening wore on, Emma noticed a shift in the family dynamic. The conversations seemed to have more depth and more genuine emotion. Even her usually stoic father opened up about his concerns for his retirement, leading to a supportive discussion about financial planning and family support.

Driving home that night, Emma felt a warmth in her chest that had nothing to do with the glass of wine she'd had with dinner. She realized that by choosing authenticity, she hadn't just changed her own experience – she'd created space for others to be more genuine as well.

As she got ready for bed, Emma reflected on the past twenty-four hours. It hadn't been easy, and there had been moments of doubt and discomfort. But the connections she'd made, the genuine interactions she'd experienced, far outweighed any temporary unease.

She knew that this was just the beginning of her journey towards a more authentic life. There would be challenges ahead, situations where being genuine might be met with resistance or misunderstanding. But Emma felt equipped to face those challenges now, armed with the knowledge of how transformative true authenticity could be.

As she drifted off to sleep, Emma felt a sense of peace she hadn't experienced in years. For the first time in a long time, she felt truly aligned with herself – no mask, no pretense, just Emma. And that, she realized, was the most powerful thing of all.

In our increasingly interconnected yet often superficial world, the value of genuineness and authenticity cannot be overstated. Being true to oneself and presenting an honest face to the world is not just a matter of personal integrity; it has far-reaching implications for our mental health, relationships, and overall quality of life.

Why Authenticity Matters

1. Mental Health and Well-being: Living authentically allows us to align our actions with our values and beliefs, reducing internal conflict and stress. When we constantly put on a facade or try to be someone we're not, we create a dissonance within ourselves that can lead to anxiety, depression, and a sense of unfulfillment. By embracing our true selves, we cultivate self-acceptance and self-esteem, which are crucial components of good mental health.

2. Deeper, More Meaningful Relationships: Authenticity fosters trust and intimacy in our relationships. When we present our genuine selves to others, we create opportunities for real connections. People are drawn to authenticity because it makes them feel safe to be themselves as well. This mutual openness can lead to more supportive, understanding, and fulfilling relationships, both personal and professional.

3. Improved Decision Making: When we're in touch with our true selves, we make decisions that are more aligned with our values and goals. This leads to choices that are more likely to bring us satisfaction and success in the long run. Authenticity helps us cut through societal expectations and peer pressure to focus on what truly matters to us.

4. Increased Creativity and Productivity: Authenticity allows us to tap into our unique perspectives and ideas. When we're not constrained by trying to fit into a mold or meet others' expectations, we're free to explore our true passions and talents. This can lead to increased creativity, innovation, and productivity in both our personal and professional lives.

5. Leadership and Influence: Authentic individuals often make the most effective leaders. Their genuineness inspires trust and respect from others. In a world where people are increasingly skeptical of authority figures, authentic leadership stands out and has the power to motivate and influence others positively.

6. Reduced Stress and Increased Resilience: Maintaining a false persona is exhausting. When we live authentically, we conserve the mental and emotional energy that would otherwise be spent on keeping up appearances. This leaves us with more resources to handle life's challenges, increasing our resilience in the face of adversity.

7. Personal Growth and Self-Awareness: The journey towards authenticity is also a journey of self-discovery. As we strive to be more genuine, we learn more about ourselves - our strengths, weaknesses, values, and desires. This self-awareness is the foundation for personal growth and continuous improvement.

How to Be Genuine and Authentic

Now that we understand why authenticity is so important let's explore how we can cultivate it in our lives:

1. Self-Reflection and Self-Awareness: The journey to authenticity begins with knowing yourself. Take time regularly to reflect on your thoughts, feelings, values, and motivations. Ask yourself:

- What truly matters to me?
- What are my core values?
- What brings me joy and fulfillment?
- What are my strengths and weaknesses?

Consider keeping a journal to track your thoughts and feelings. This can help you identify patterns and gain insights into your authentic self.

2. Identify and Challenge Your Masks: We all wear masks in different situations. While some of these may be necessary for social functioning, others might be holding us back from true authenticity. Try to identify the personas you adopt in different settings - at work, with family, with friends. Ask yourself:

- Why do I put on this mask?
- What am I afraid would happen if I didn't?
- Is this mask serving me, or is it limiting me?

Once you've identified your masks, challenge them. Start small by letting your guard down in safe situations and see what happens.

3. Practice Honesty and Transparency: Authenticity requires honesty - with yourself and with others. This doesn't mean being brutally blunt but rather communicating your thoughts, feelings, and intentions clearly and respectfully. When you make a mistake, own up to it. When you're struggling, don't be afraid to ask for help. When you disagree with someone, express your perspective kindly but firmly.

4. Align Your Actions with Your Values: Identify your core values and make a conscious effort to align your actions with them. This might mean making tough choices or going against the grain sometimes. But when your actions reflect your true beliefs, you'll feel more authentic and at peace with yourself.

5. Embrace Your Uniqueness: Each of us has a unique combination of traits, experiences, and perspectives. Instead of trying to fit in or be like someone else, celebrate what makes you different. Your quirks, your unusual interests, your distinctive way of seeing the world - these are all part of your authentic self.

6. Practice Self-Acceptance: Authenticity doesn't mean perfection. It means accepting yourself, flaws, and all. Recognize that everyone has strengths and weaknesses, and it's the combination of these that makes us human. Practice self-compassion and treat yourself with the same kindness you would offer a good friend.

7. Set Boundaries: Being authentic means honoring your own needs and limits. Learn to say no to things that don't align with your values or that overextend you. Communicate your boundaries clearly and respectfully to others.

8. Surround Yourself with Supportive People: It's easier to be authentic when you're around people who accept and appreciate you for who you are. Seek out relationships with people who encourage you to be yourself and who respond positively to your authenticity.

9. Practice Vulnerability: Being authentic often means allowing yourself to be vulnerable. This can be scary, but it's also the pathway to deeper connections and personal growth. Start small by sharing something personal with a trusted friend or by admitting when you're unsure or need help.

10. Live in the Present: Authenticity happens in the present moment. Practice mindfulness to stay connected with your current thoughts, feelings, and surroundings. This can help you respond more genuinely to situations as they arise rather than falling back on habitual or inauthentic behaviors.

11. Continuously Reassess and Adjust: Authenticity is not a destination but a journey. As you grow and change, your authentic self may evolve too. Regularly check in with yourself to ensure that your actions and choices still align with your current values and goals.

12. Be Patient with Yourself: Becoming more authentic is a process that takes time. You may face setbacks or find yourself falling into old patterns. That's okay. Be patient and kind to yourself as you learn and grow.

13. Express Yourself Creatively: Creative expression can be a powerful tool for authenticity. Whether it's through art, writing, music, or any other medium, find ways to express your true self creatively. This can help you connect with your authentic voice and share it with others.

14. Practice Authentic Communication: Work on expressing yourself clearly and honestly in your communications. This includes not just your words but also your tone of voice, body language, and actions. Strive for congruence between what you say and how you say it.

15. Challenge Your Fear of Judgment: Often, what holds us back from being authentic is the fear of being judged by others. Remember that you can't control others' opinions, and trying to do so only leads you away from your true self. Focus instead on being true to yourself and let go of the need for universal approval.

16. Develop Your Own Moral Compass: Rather than blindly following societal norms or others' expectations, take the time to develop your own sense of right and wrong. This internal moral compass will guide you toward more authentic choices and actions.

17. Practice Self-Care: Taking care of your physical, emotional, and mental health is crucial for authenticity. When you're run down or stressed, it's harder to stay true to yourself. Prioritize self-care activities that genuinely nurture and replenish you.

18. Embrace Change and Growth: Authenticity doesn't mean rigidly sticking to one way of being. As you learn and grow, allow your authentic self to evolve. Be open to new experiences and perspectives that can enrich your understanding of yourself and the world.

19. Seek Feedback, But Trust Yourself: While it's valuable to consider others' perspectives, remember that you are the ultimate authority on your authentic self. Seek feedback from trusted sources, but always filter it through your own values and self-knowledge.

20. Practice Gratitude: Regularly acknowledging what you're grateful for can help you stay connected to what truly matters to you. This, in turn, can guide you toward more authentic choices and behaviors.

Chapter 6: Find Common Ground

Identify a shared interest, a local event, or a unique aspect of your surroundings to initiate a conversation, just like finding a beautiful seashell on the beach.

Now that you've greeted them with warmth and charm (hopefully), the real work begins - sustaining the conversation in a positive way. The way to keep discussions lively and flowing is to find common ground.

Finding common ground with someone is a powerful way to strengthen connections and foster deeper relationships. Discovering shared interests, values, or experiences creates a sense of familiarity and understanding. This chapter explores ways to find common ground with people you don't know and leverage it to build stronger, more meaningful connections.

Now, imagine yourself strolling around the park for a moment when something interesting catches your eye—a person sitting by themselves playing with their dog, a friendly-looking mutt. Not wanting them to feel alone, you approach and say, "What a cute pup! May I pet them?"

The person lights up at your greeting. "Of course, her name is Daisy," the person replies. You bend down to give Daisy some loving scratches behind the ears. "She's such a sweetie. I've always had a soft spot for dogs," you remark.

"Me too; they're the best companions," they agree. Soon, you find yourselves immersed in a discussion about your canine loves. You learn that Buddy, your Labrador, loves to fetch more than any other game. Daisy, on the other hand, prefers cuddles to exercise.

The conversation flows as you compare tricks your pups have learned over the years. Imitating a few hand signals, you each have the other laughing at your dog's antics. Daisy even joins in the fun by rolling over on cue, begging for extra belly rubs from her new friend.

Naturally, the exchange progresses to care routines. Laughing, you realize you both struggle with shedding season each spring. Regular brushing helps, but fur still finds its way everywhere! At least your pups are worth it. Grooming segues into favorite parks to walk and play.

Somehow, your lively chat shifts to travels. To your surprise, they have visited the same city you just crossed off your bucket list - Portland, Maine. For over half an hour, you rave about the charming waterfront, delicious seafood, and cozy coffee shops nestled in every corner.

Your discussion touches on favorite discoveries from your visits to Portland. Laughing over photos from the renowned Arts District, you notice one of their pictures features street sculptures.

"Wow, the detail in that carved mermaid is stunning," you remark. They nod appreciatively, zooming in on intricate etchings around the sculpture.

"I love how artists can transform solid materials into motion. It actually inspires my sculptures at times," they say almost shyly.

Turning to them with interest, you ask them to share more. They pull out pictures of their recent works and describe their creative process.

"I'd love to see your pieces sometime," you tell them sincerely.

As the afternoon winds down, you exchange numbers, set a date, and part ways, feeling uplifted by this chance meeting and looking forward to a newfound friendship blossoming.

Who knew where a simple hello to an adorable pup would lead?

So now you can see that finding common ground is a significant factor in making connections.

In some cases, it'll be more obvious, such as two people being dog owners; in other cases, it may be more subtle, like their appreciation for fine art.

Here are some ways you can find common ground.

Shared Hobbies and Interests: Explore common hobbies or interests you enjoy. Whether it's a love for a particular sport, a shared passion for a hobby like painting or cooking, or an interest in a specific genre of music or literature, finding common ground in these areas can provide a solid foundation for further discussion and connection.

Personal Experiences: Share personal experiences and stories that relate to the topic at hand. When you open up about your own experiences, it encourages the other person to do the same. Look for similarities or shared challenges in your stories, as these can create a sense of empathy and understanding.

Values and Beliefs: Discuss values and beliefs that are important to both of you. These can be shared ethical principles, a commitment to certain causes or social issues, or a similar outlook on life. Recognizing shared values can deepen the connection and foster a sense of alignment.

Current Events and Pop Culture: Staying informed about current events, popular culture, and other trends can effectively form connections. These topics often provide a common ground for discussion. Whether it's the latest movies, TV shows, books, or news stories, being knowledgeable about these subjects can help initiate conversations and find shared interests.

Travel and Experiences: Share travel experiences or places you both have visited. Talk about the places you've been, the cultures you've experienced, and the memorable moments you've had. Finding common destinations or shared experiences can spark engaging conversations and create a bond.

Professional or Educational Background: Explore commonalities in your professional or educational backgrounds. Discuss common industries, areas of expertise, or educational experiences. These shared experiences can provide a starting point for meaningful conversations and a deeper understanding of each other's perspectives.

Mutual Connections: Discover mutual connections or acquaintances. It could be someone you both know personally or a shared connection through social media or professional networks. Shared connections can serve as a bridge for conversation and provide common ground for discussion.

Collaboration and Shared Goals: Identify opportunities for collaboration or shared goals. If you're both passionate about a particular cause or interested in achieving similar objectives, working together can strengthen your connection and create a sense of purpose.

Cultural and Heritage Backgrounds: Explore each other's cultural or heritage backgrounds. Discuss traditions, customs, or cuisines that are meaningful to both of you. Sharing and learning about each other's cultural backgrounds can create a deeper appreciation and understanding.

Now, here are some things to remember when finding common ground:

Don't Dominate the Conversation: Dominating the conversation can make the other person feel unheard and unimportant. Give them space to express themselves and actively listen to what they have to say. Engage in a balanced dialogue that allows both parties to contribute and share their perspectives.

Don't Make Assumptions: Assuming you know someone's interests, experiences, or beliefs without allowing them to express themselves can lead to misunderstandings. Give them the opportunity to share their thoughts and experiences organically without imposing your own assumptions or judgments.

Don't Force Common Ground: Authentic connections are built on genuine shared interests and experiences. Trying to force common ground by pretending to have interests or experiences you don't truly resonate with will only create a superficial connection. Be true to yourself and find common ground that aligns with your genuine interests.

Don't Dismiss or Invalidate Differing Opinions: Respecting differing opinions is crucial for meaningful conversations. Dismissing or invalidating someone's viewpoint can shut down the dialogue and create a sense of hostility. Instead, strive for respectful dialogue, seeking to understand their perspective even if you don't agree with it.

Don't Focus Solely on Yourself: Engaging in a one-sided conversation centered solely on your own interests and experiences can alienate the other person. Show genuine interest in their thoughts, experiences, and perspectives. Actively listen and create a space where both parties feel valued and heard.

Don't Rush the Process: Building common ground takes time. Avoid rushing the conversation or expecting instant connections. Allow the dialogue to unfold naturally, giving both parties the opportunity to share their stories and interests at a comfortable pace. Patience and genuine curiosity will foster deeper connections.

Don't Engage in Heated Debates: While healthy debates can be enriching, turning conversations into heated arguments can damage relationships. Maintain a respectful and open-minded approach, focusing on finding common ground rather than trying to prove someone wrong. Create an environment where differing opinions can be discussed without hostility.

Remember, the goal is not to force common ground but to genuinely find areas of shared interest and connection. Building on common ground can lead to more meaningful and enjoyable interactions with people, especially those you don't know.

Chapter 7: Respect Personal Boundaries

Respect others' personal space like a captain respects the sea. If they seem uninterested, gracefully move on as the tide ebbs away. Prioritize the environment and situation before approaching someone, just as a captain considers weather and sea conditions before setting sail. Always respect their boundaries and comfort, adapting your approach based on the context and their responses.

Eli walked into the busy coffee shop in the midday rush. He got in line to order his usual latte and spotted an empty table in the corner. As he made his way over carrying his drink, he noticed a woman sitting by herself reading a book. She had dark hair pulled back into a ponytail and looked deep in concentration. Something made Eli want to try chatting with her, as she seemed interesting.

Eli took a deep breath and approached her table. "Excuse me, do you mind if I sit here? Everywhere else is full."

She looked up and nodded. "Sure, go ahead."

He sat down across from her with his drink.

"Thanks! I'm Eli, by the way."

She gave a small smile. "Jennifer."

Eli noticed she had a French accent. "You're not from around here?"

She shook her head. "No, I just moved from Paris last month for a new job."

"Wow, Paris, that's amazing! What brought you all the way to Seattle?"

She hesitated before responding, "I'm working for a fashion design company here now." Her answer seemed curt.

Eli pressed on anyway, figuring she might warm up. "Fashion design, very cool. Do you miss Paris at all?"

She shrugged. "Some things, but it's nice for a change."

Okay, one-word answers. Not a great sign. But Eli wasn't ready to give up yet.

"Have you had a chance to explore Seattle yet? There are some great parks and museums you should check out if you like being outdoors." She nodded again but didn't offer any suggestions for follow-up questions.

Thinking quickly, Eli changed his strategy. "So, what book are you reading? Anything good?"

She tilted it toward him to see the cover but didn't say the title. "It's alright."

Yikes, this was not going well. She was clearly sending signals she was not interested in chatting. Eli decided it was time to cut his losses.

"Well, it was nice meeting you, Jennifer, but I'll let you get back to your book. Enjoy the rest of your afternoon!"

She nodded and, with a quick "Thanks," turned her attention back to the pages in front of her without making eye contact.

We've all been in situations where we've wished to strike up a friendly conversation with a stranger. However, initiating interactions requires sensitivity to the other person's comfort level and willingness to engage. Not respecting personal boundaries can potentially make the situation awkward or even stressful for the other individual.

Eli found himself at a local coffee shop, hoping to meet someone new. As Eli waited in line, he spotted a woman sitting alone reading and thought she seemed like someone he'd like to get to know. However, upon approaching her table, Eli failed to gauge her receptiveness to the conversation properly.

While she politely allowed Eli to sit, he missed the subtle cues that she really just wanted peace and quiet to enjoy her book. Her short, disinterested responses should have been a red flag, but Eli pushed on, not wanting to accept the disinterest. By staying longer than welcomed, Eli risked making her feel uneasy or annoyed by his persistence.

Everyone deserves to have their personal space and boundaries respected. Approaching interactions with that understanding is respectful. With practice, Eli has learned to pay closer attention to subtle body language and vocal tones that indicate interest level before engaging.

Things like how quickly someone responds, the depth of their answers, eye contact, and posture can subtly express eagerness or unease. While intentions may have been friendly, not respecting those signals risks coming across as disregarding or inconsiderate of the other person's comfort. We must avoid that at all costs to build trust.

Respecting others' personal boundaries is important in social interactions, especially when approaching people you don't know. No one enjoys feeling like another person is invading their space or that their signals of discomfort are being ignored. However, many people are not always attuned to subtle cues regarding boundaries.

People naturally feel uneasy when someone enters their personal space without invitation. This invisible boundary can vary between cultures and individuals. As a general rule, one must maintain an arm's length distance initially.

Observe body language - is the person leaning away, fidgeting, or making direct eye contact? If so, give more space. In some settings like elevators or crowded bars, closer proximity may be warranted, but remain aware.

Personal boundaries are highly subjective. Factors like gender, neurodivergence, past trauma, and culture shape individual definitions of personal space. Those with anxiety or on the autism spectrum may find most social interactions overwhelming.

Beyond invading their personal space, learn to read cues that indicate interest or discomfort. Make eye contact and note if it is held or if the person looks away. Maintaining eye contact shows active listening and interest in the discussion.

Listen to the tone of voice, word choice, and details in the responses. Enthusiasm comes through clearly in long, descriptive answers. One or two-word replies without further prompting likely mean disinterest. If sarcasm or displeasure creeps into nonverbal sounds or facial expressions, it's best to move the conversation in a positive direction or wrap it up respectfully.

Physically entering someone's personal bubble without asking first is disrespectful. If approaching someone in a public place, ask, "Do you mind if I join you?" before sitting next to a stranger in the park. Respect goes both ways - do not feel offended if denied. As with proximity, subtle cues can hint if physical distance needs adjusting.

Another thing to consider is if others seem relaxed or in a hurry. Matching their level of energy, formality, and topics shows consideration. Talking passionately on a complex issue may overwhelm a weary commuter. Keep responses engaging but not draining for them.

Provide outs when initiating contact to avoid putting undue pressure on the other person. It's important to provide them with an easy way to withdraw comfortably if they seem unreceptive. Introduce yourself, ask a question, and follow with "No pressure if you'd rather not chat." If they seem unresponsive, thank them for their time and take your leave gracefully without pushback. This validates their boundaries while maintaining courtesy.

Now, it can be easy to take their disinterest personally. But the truth is, it usually has more to do with them than you. So don't sweat it!

There could be a million reasons why someone isn't feeling chatty at the moment... maybe they're stressed, in a rush, or just feeling introverted. It's nothing personal. People are complex, and you never know what's going on in their lives. Chances are it has nothing to do with your likability.

Besides, would you really want to force a conversation with someone who so clearly isn't in the mood?

Respect their boundaries and give them space. That respects both people's energy. And who knows, maybe next time, the circumstances will be different, and they'll be more receptive!

Instead of focusing on the people who aren't feeling it, appreciate the ones who light up at the chance to connect. Enjoy those interactions that match the energy that you give out.

Chapter 8: The Art of Asking Questions

In life, conversations often resemble navigating an unpredictable sea. Knowing when to ride the waves of curiosity and when to let the currents of understanding guide you is essential. Just as a sailor adjusts their sails to catch the wind, we must learn to ask questions that bring depth, insight, and meaning to our conversations.

The lunchtime rush at the café was in full swing as Ava grabbed the last open table. As she sat down with her salad, a young man nearby, Eli, scanned the room and approached her.

"Excuse me, is this seat taken?" he asked, gesturing to the empty chair across from her.

"No, it's free," Ava replied, nodding.

The man sat down, giving her a friendly smile. "I'm Eli, by the way."

"Hi, I'm Ava," she said, taking a bite of her salad.

"So, do you come here often?" Eli asked.

"Uh, sometimes," Ava responded, her mouth still full.

"What do you usually get?" Eli continued.

"The salad," Ava said, swallowing.

Eli nodded, but the conversation seemed to stall. After a moment of awkward silence, he tried again.

"Do you work around here?"

"Yes, in an office a few blocks away," Ava replied.

Another pause. Eli fidgeted with his napkin, struggling to keep the conversation going.

"That's cool. What do you do?"

"I'm an accountant," Ava said, taking another bite.

Eli nodded again, his brow furrowing slightly. He could tell Ava wasn't exactly thrilled to be chatting with him.

"Do you enjoy your work?" he asked, hoping to find a more engaging topic.

"It's okay, I guess," Ava shrugged.

The interaction was starting to feel more like an interrogation than a natural conversation. Eli could sense Ava's disinterest and decided not to pry further.

The problem was that Eli had led the conversation with a series of closed-ended questions, which clearly did him no favors.

By asking things like "Do you come here often?" and "What do you usually get?" he was essentially putting Ava on the spot, eliciting short, one-word responses that did little to further the dialogue.

These types of closed-ended questions are like conversational dead ends. They don't leave much room for the other person to share their thoughts, experiences, and perspectives. Instead, they tend to trap the conversation in a cycle of basic information exchange, with little opportunity for deeper exploration or connection.

As Eli continued down this path, pressing Ava with questions about her work and whether she enjoyed it, the interaction only grew more strained. Ava's responses became increasingly curt and disengaged, and the pauses between them grew longer and more awkward.

Eli could feel the conversation dragging like they were stuck in conversational quicksand. No matter how hard he tried to keep it going, the interaction lacked any real spark or momentum. It was clear that his reliance on closed-ended questions was not serving him well.

Now, imagine if Eli had instead led with open-ended questions. When he sat down, he could have started with: "So, what brings you to this café today? Are you a regular here or just passing through?" This small change created a warm, open environment, encouraging Ava to reveal more about herself. She mentioned her job nearby and her enjoyment of the café's atmosphere.

Eli nodded, genuinely interested. "That's great. What do you do for work, if you don't mind me asking?"

"I'm an accountant," Ava said and then paused as if expecting Eli to ask a more specific follow-up question.

Sensing an opportunity, Eli leaned in slightly and asked, "Ah, an accountant – that must be a fascinating field. What do you enjoy most about your work?" Ava responded with enthusiasm, sharing her love for problem-solving in her accounting role. Eli listened attentively, and the conversation naturally.

Eventually, Ava paused and looked at Eli. "What about you? What do you do for a living?"

Eli smiled, pleased that the interaction had shifted to a more balanced dialogue. "Actually, I work in the tech industry, but I have to say, your job sounds a lot more interesting than mine at the moment. I'd love to hear more about the ins and outs of being an accountant if you're willing to share."

The two continued their conversation, discovering common flowed into deeper topics, revealing shared interests and creating a sense of connection. By starting with open-ended questions that invited Ava to share her perspectives and experiences, Eli was able to create a welcoming environment where she felt comfortable opening up.

The two continued their conversation, discovering common interests and building a sense of connection. By starting with open-ended questions that invited Ava to share her perspectives and experiences, Eli was able to create a welcoming environment where she felt comfortable opening up.

In our daily interactions, the way we ask questions can shape the depth and quality of our connections. By refining the art of questioning, we turn ordinary exchanges into opportunities for understanding, insight, and even transformation. Whether with friends, colleagues, or strangers, thoughtful questions unlock layers of meaning, leading to richer, more fulfilling relationships.

In the previous chapter, we discussed the importance of respecting personal boundaries when approaching new people. Striking the right balance between engaging and respecting space is crucial for building trust and rapport.

Open-ended questions are an incredibly valuable tool when it comes to approaching and engaging with new people. Here's why they can be so effective:

Encourages Sharing and Openness

By asking open-ended questions, you're inviting the other person to share more about themselves, their thoughts, and their experiences. Questions that begin with "what," "how," "why," or "tell me about" encourage a more detailed, expansive response compared to closed-ended questions that can be answered with a simple "yes," "no," or one-word reply.

This subtle difference creates a welcoming environment where the other person feels heard and empowered to open up at their own pace. Open-ended questions convey genuine interest and a willingness to listen, which can put the person at ease and make them more inclined to engage in a meaningful exchange.

Uncovers Interests and Perspectives

When you ask open-ended questions, you give the other person the opportunity to share what's truly important to them. You might learn about their passions, goals, and values - insights that can help you find common ground and build a real connection.

Closed-ended questions, on the other hand, often only scratch the surface, limiting the conversation to basic facts and details. Open-ended questions allow the other person's unique personality, interests, and perspectives to shine through, giving you a richer understanding of who they are.

Demonstrates Respect and Curiosity

By leading with open-ended questions, you signal to the other person that you respect their autonomy and are genuinely curious about their experiences. This conveys an attitude of openness and a willingness to learn rather than an agenda to gather information or steer the conversation in a predetermined direction.

This respectful approach can help put the other person at ease, making them more receptive to engaging with you. It shows that you value their input and perspectives, which can be particularly important when approaching someone you don't know well.

Encourages a Collaborative Dialogue

Open-ended questions naturally facilitate a more balanced, back-and-forth conversation. Rather than an interrogation-style exchange, open-ended questions allow the discussion to flow organically, with both parties contributing and building on each other's ideas.

This collaborative dynamic can help establish a sense of rapport and mutual understanding. It creates an environment where both people feel heard, respected, and invested in the conversation.

Mastering the Art of Asking Questions

While open-ended questions can create a welcoming environment for conversation, it's important to recognize that some people may still choose to keep their responses brief or guarded, even in the face of a positive, inviting approach.

When we lead with open-ended questions, we're essentially handing the other person the conversational reins and giving them control over how much they want to share. This can be a powerful way to build rapport and foster genuine connection. However, we have to be mindful that not everyone will reciprocate that openness, even if they are being "nice" on the surface.

Some people may have their own reasons for maintaining a certain distance or level of formality in their interactions - whether it's due to shyness, a reserved personality, or simply a preference for more shallow conversation. By asking open-ended questions, we invite them to go deeper, but they may decline that invitation, even if they're outwardly polite.

This is an important nuance to understand. Just because someone responds positively to your greeting and initial questions doesn't necessarily mean they're fully engaged or interested in a more substantive exchange. They may simply be adhering to social norms and etiquette without any real desire to open up or connect on a deeper level.

The key is to pay attention to subtle cues and be respectful of each person's comfort level and boundaries. If you notice the other person responding with short, perfunctory answers, even after you've posed open-ended questions, that may be a sign that they're not particularly eager to dive into a more in-depth discussion.

In those cases, it's important to respect their wishes and not try to force the conversation further. You can acknowledge their responses, perhaps with a lighthearted comment, and then gracefully move the interaction in a different direction or bring it to a close. The goal is to create a positive experience for both parties, not to coerce someone into a level of vulnerability they're not ready for.

By being attuned to these dynamics, you can strike a balance between extending an open, welcoming invitation and respecting the other person's personal boundaries. Open-ended questions are powerful, but they work best when paired with a keen sense of social awareness and a willingness to adapt your approach based on the other person's comfort and responsiveness.

The art of asking questions involves more than choosing between open and closed formats. Here are key strategies to deepen connections through thoughtful questioning:

1. Know When to Use Different Types of Questions: Closed-ended questions can confirm facts or clarify details, but open-ended questions are vital when the goal is to connect and engage. A balance between both keeps the conversation dynamic.

2. Be Attuned to Responses: Pay attention to engagement cues. If someone seems reserved, start with lighter questions and gauge their willingness to go deeper. Adapt your approach based on their responses for a comfortable exchange.

3. Show Curiosity, Not an Agenda: True curiosity fosters a more genuine conversation. Avoid steering with an agenda, and focus instead on exploring who they are and what matters to them.

4. Use Follow-Up Questions: Follow-ups like "How did you get into that?" or "What do you enjoy most about it?" demonstrate interest and allow for richer discussions that reveal unique perspectives.

5. Respect Boundaries: If someone responds tersely or seems reserved, respect their pace. Redirect the conversation lightly, keeping it pleasant without pressing too hard.

Advanced Techniques for Deeper Connection

Beyond initial exchanges, asking questions that foster deeper dialogue transforms simple exchanges into memorable interactions.

1. Mirroring and Paraphrasing: Echoing language or ideas someone expresses shows you're listening and creates rapport. For example, Eli might mirror Ava's words about problem-solving to make her feel understood.

2. Empathetic Statements Before Questions: Prefacing questions with empathetic statements like, "It sounds like your work can be demanding and rewarding," validates their experience and encourages openness.

3. Mind the Tone and Body Language: Tone and body language set the stage for responses. An open, relaxed posture and warm tone convey friendliness and make even personal questions feel inviting.

4. Mindful Pauses: Silence can encourage thoughtful responses. Giving a few moments after asking "What do you enjoy most about your work?" allows the other person to respond naturally.

5. Invite Stories, Not Facts: Frame questions that invite storytelling, like "What was one of your favorite memories from school?" to shift from facts to richer, more personal conversations.

6. Frame Questions with Positive Assumptions: Positive assumptions, such as "What's a recent project you're proud of?" create an uplifting atmosphere that naturally encourages people to open up.

7. Lean into Emotions: Dive deeper with follow-up questions about emotional experiences. If someone shares an achievement, asking "What did that mean to you?" invites a deeper connection to the story.

8. Acknowledge Vulnerability: When someone shares something personal, acknowledging it—"Thanks for sharing that"—fosters a trusting environment and encourages further openness.

Mastering the art of asking questions isn't about getting the "right" answers but about creating an environment of trust, curiosity, and connection. By allowing for silence, respecting boundaries, and choosing questions thoughtfully, we invite others into a journey of shared discovery. Well-placed questions turn everyday conversations into memorable encounters, where both parties leave feeling seen, heard, and valued. In the vast ocean of communication, questions become the compass that guides us toward genuine human understanding.

The art of asking questions ultimately transforms interactions into genuine exchanges of ideas, experiences, and feelings. As we become attuned to others' unique ways of engaging, we learn that true connection isn't about what we ask but how we listen and respond. Well-placed, thoughtful questions can turn a simple conversation into a memorable moment, helping us connect on a level that transcends words.

In the end, asking questions is less about finding answers and more about creating shared understanding. Whether in brief encounters or deep conversations, each question we ask shapes the conversation's course. By inviting others to share and respecting their responses, we foster a rich dialogue that reveals the humanity in each of us, one question at a time.

Chapter 9: Practice Active Listening

Show genuine interest in their responses by maintaining eye contact and asking follow-up questions, like a sailor attentively reading the ocean's currents.

Eli scanned the crowded stadium, and his eyes landed on a man wearing a vintage Jerome Bettis jersey from the Steelers' glory days. A smile spread across Eli's face as he approached the stranger.

"Excuse me, great jersey, man! Bettis was an absolute beast back in the day," Eli said, his tone warm and genuine.

The man looked up, a bit surprised by the friendly greeting. "Oh, hey there! Yeah, this old thing has been a game-day staple for me since I was a kid. I've been a Steelers fan my whole life."

"That's awesome," Eli replied. "I'm a huge Steelers fan too. What do you think about their chances this season? I'm really hoping they can make a deep playoff run, especially with that defense they've got."

The man's face lit up as Eli showed genuine interest. "Well, you know, I think they've got a shot if the offense can find a little more consistency. The defense has been carrying them, but they're going to need a few more playmakers to step up on that side of the ball, you know?"

Eli nodded enthusiastically. "Absolutely, I agree. The quarterback has been a little up and down lately. But hey, what do you think about that new offensive coordinator they brought in? I'm curious to see how he shakes things up."

The two men launched into a lively discussion about the team's strengths, weaknesses, and the potential impact of the coaching changes. Eli was fully engaged, asking open-ended questions and keeping his attention focused on the stranger's responses.

As their conversation continued, Eli's gaze occasionally drifted toward the field, where the players were starting to warm up. He caught a glimpse of a highlight reel from the previous game playing on the jumbotron, and his mind momentarily wandered.

The man noticed Eli's distraction and paused mid-sentence. "Hey, am I keeping you from something? I can tell the game is about to start, and I don't want to hold you up."

Eli snapped back to attention, realizing he had let his focus slip. "No, no, not at all! I'm really enjoying talking football with you. It's just..." He trailed off, searching for the right words. "Sometimes, there's just so much going on that it's easy for my mind to wander. But please, go on. I'm listening, I promise."

The man nodded, but Eli could see a slight shift in his demeanor. The two continued their conversation, but Eli found it increasingly difficult to maintain the same level of engagement and attentiveness as before.

Eventually, the man glanced at his watch and said, "Well, I better get going. Looks like the game is about to start, and I don't want to miss the kick-off. It was great chatting with you, though. Enjoy the game!"

Eli watched as the man walked away, feeling a pang of regret. He had started the interaction so well, finding common ground and keeping the dialogue flowing with open-ended questions.

But his inability to fully focus on the conversation had undermined the connection he had started to build.

It was a humbling experience for Eli, a reminder that active listening, even in the midst of a bustling, high-energy environment, requires constant practice and discipline. As he turned his attention back to the field, Eli made a mental note to be more mindful of his focus and presence in future interactions with strangers.

In our fast-paced world, the art of true listening has become a rare and invaluable skill. It's tempting to constantly multitask, to half-listen while mentally formulating our next response. However, if we want to build genuine connections and have rewarding conversations, active listening must be a priority.

Active listening goes far beyond simply hearing the words someone says. It requires being fully present and tuned in to both the verbal and nonverbal cues they're providing. When we actively listen, we demonstrate that the other person's thoughts, feelings, and experiences are worthy of our undivided attention. This creates an environment of trust, respect, and mutual understanding - the foundation for meaningful relationships.

The Importance of Active Listening

There are numerous benefits to honing the skill of active listening. First and foremost, it shows the speaker that they are valued. Too often, people feel ignored, dismissed, or unheard in their daily interactions. By practicing active listening, we convey that their perspective matters and that we are eager to understand them truly.

This validation can have a profound impact. When someone feels truly heard, it can open them up, encouraging them to share more deeply and authentically. Active listening fosters a sense of psychological safety, allowing the conversation to evolve into a rich, collaborative exchange of ideas and experiences.

Beyond strengthening interpersonal bonds, active listening also has cognitive benefits. By resisting the urge to formulate our own responses while someone is speaking, we free up mental bandwidth to fully process and comprehend the information they're providing. This can lead to better retention, deeper insights, and more thoughtful, well-informed replies.

Moreover, active listening helps us avoid misunderstandings and incorrect assumptions. When we're solely focused on our own agenda or internal dialogue, we're more likely to misinterpret the speaker's meaning or overlook crucial details. But by staying present and attuned, we can gain a nuanced, textured understanding of their perspective.

Mastering the Art of Active Listening

So, how does one become a more active listener? It starts with making a conscious choice to be fully engaged in the conversation rather than letting our minds wander. Here are some key practices to cultivate:

Maintain eye contact. Keeping your gaze on the speaker demonstrates that you are focused on them and their message. Avoid the temptation to glance around the room or down at your phone.

Use positive body language. Lean in slightly, nod your head, and adopt an open, attentive posture. These nonverbal cues convey your interest and encouragement.

Resist interrupting. It can be tempting to jump in with a response or related anecdote, but try to resist the urge. Allow the speaker to fully express their thoughts before formulating your own.

Ask clarifying questions. When the speaker pauses, use open-ended questions to prompt them to elaborate. This shows you're listening closely and wanting to gain a deeper understanding.

Paraphrase and summarize. Occasionally, reflect on what you've heard by paraphrasing key points or summarizing the main themes. This demonstrates your comprehension and gives the speaker a chance to correct any misunderstandings.

Avoid internal distractions. It's normal for our minds to wander occasionally, especially in busy or stimulating environments. When you notice your attention drifting, gently bring it back to the present moment and the person speaking.

Mastering these active listening skills takes practice, but the payoffs are immense. When we make a choice to be fully present and engaged, we create an atmosphere of trust, openness, and mutual respect. The speaker feels heard, validated, and encouraged to share more.

Common Pitfalls to Avoid

Of course, active listening is not without its challenges. There are certain behaviors and mindsets that can undermine our efforts and derail the conversation. Being aware of these pitfalls is crucial.

One common mistake is allowing ourselves to get distracted by external stimuli. Whether it's glancing at our phones, scanning the room, or becoming preoccupied with background noises, these diversions pull our focus away from the speaker. We must consciously reign in our wandering attention and re-center ourselves in the present moment.

Another pitfall is the tendency to formulate our responses while the other person is still speaking. Instead of truly listening, we're often busy planning what we're going to say next. This not only prevents us from fully comprehending their message but can also cause us to miss important nuances or opportunities to ask clarifying questions.

Additionally, we must be wary of making assumptions or jumping to conclusions. Active listening requires an open, curious mindset, free from preconceived notions. When we make snap judgments or fill in the blanks, we risk misunderstanding the speaker's true meaning and perspective.

Lastly, it's crucial to avoid interrupting or monopolizing the conversation. While it's tempting to interject with our own thoughts and experiences, doing so can make the speaker feel unheard or dismissed. We must resist the urge to redirect the dialogue and instead allow it to flow organically.

Chapter 10: Show Empathy and Understanding

Dive beneath the surface of words and seek to understand the currents of emotions and perspectives.

Eli trudged into the coffee shop; his shoulders slumped under the weight of a particularly grueling day at work. As he approached the counter, he noticed the barista—a young woman with vibrant blue hair—looked equally worn down.

"Large coffee, black," Eli mumbled, barely making eye contact.

The barista nodded silently and turned to prepare his order. As she worked, Eli's gaze drifted to her nametag: "Sophie." He couldn't help but notice her hands trembling slightly as she poured the coffee.

When Sophie returned with his drink, Eli paused before taking it. "Rough day?" he asked softly.

Sophie's eyes widened in surprise, then softened. "Is it that obvious?" she replied with a weak smile.

Eli shrugged. "Takes one to know one, I guess."

For a moment, they shared a look of mutual understanding. Then Sophie glanced at the line forming behind Eli and sighed. "Well, thanks for noticing. Enjoy your coffee."

As Eli moved to find a seat, he felt a subtle shift in his mood. The brief exchange had lifted some of the heaviness from his spirit. He settled into a corner table, sipping his coffee and observing the ebb and flow of customers.

A few minutes later, a commotion near the counter caught his attention. An irate customer was berating Sophie over what appeared to be a minor mistake in his order.

"I said soy milk, not almond milk!" the man shouted, his face reddening. "How hard is it to get a simple order right?"

Sophie stammered an apology, her earlier weariness now mixed with distress. "I'm so sorry, sir. I'll remake it right away—"

"Don't bother," the man snapped. "I don't have time for incompetence. I'll take my business elsewhere."

As the man stormed out, leaving Sophie on the verge of tears, Eli felt a surge of empathy. Without thinking, he stood and approached the counter.

"Hey," he said gently. "You okay?"

Sophie blinked rapidly, fighting back tears. "I'm fine," she muttered unconvincingly.

Eli leaned in, lowering his voice. "Listen, that guy was way out of line. You didn't deserve that."

"But he was right," Sophie whispered. "I messed up his order. I've been messing up all day. I can't seem to focus, and—" She broke off, taking a shaky breath.

Eli considered her for a moment. "Mind if I ask what's going on? Sometimes, it helps to talk."

Sophie glanced around the now-empty shop, then nodded. "My mom's in the hospital," she confessed. "She had a fall yesterday, and I've been up all night worried about her. I couldn't get anyone to cover my shift, so..." She trailed off, gesturing helplessly.

Eli felt a pang in his chest. "I'm so sorry," he said sincerely. "That must be incredibly stressful. No wonder you're having trouble concentrating."

Sophie's shoulders sagged with relief at being understood. "Yeah, it's been tough. But I can't afford to lose this job, so I'm trying to push through."

"That's really admirable," Eli said. "But also, don't be too hard on yourself. You're doing the best you can in a difficult situation."

As they talked, Eli noticed Sophie's posture gradually relaxing. The tension in her face eased, replaced by a look of cautious hope.

"Thanks for listening," she said after a while. "It means a lot."

Eli smiled. "Anytime. And hey, if you need someone to cover a shift so you can visit your mom, let me know. I used to be a barista in college—I'm sure I could manage a few hours if it would help."

Sophie's eyes widened. "Really? You'd do that for a stranger?"

"Well, we're not exactly strangers anymore, are we?" Eli replied with a wink.

As he left the coffee shop that evening, Eli realized his own troubles felt lighter. The simple act of showing empathy had not only helped Sophie but had also shifted his own perspective.

Over the next few weeks, Eli made it a point to stop by the coffee shop regularly. He covered a couple of Sophie's shifts, allowing her to spend time with her recovering mother. Their friendship grew, built on a foundation of mutual understanding and support.

One afternoon, as Eli sat working on his laptop, he overheard a conversation at a nearby table. A young man was confiding in his friend about his struggles with anxiety.

"I don't know, man," the young man said, his voice low and strained. "It's like I can't even leave my apartment some days without feeling like the world is closing in on me."

His friend shifted uncomfortably. "Have you tried, you know, just not thinking about it? Maybe if you distracted yourself more..."

Eli winced at the well-intentioned but misguided advice. He remembered his own battles with anxiety and how isolating it had felt when others didn't understand. Before he could stop himself, he turned towards their table.

"Excuse me," he said gently. "I couldn't help overhearing. I hope you don't mind, but I've dealt with anxiety too, and I just wanted to say you're not alone."

The young man looked startled, then grateful. "Really? It feels like I'm the only one sometimes."

Eli nodded empathetically. "I know that feeling. It can be really isolating. But there are people who understand, and there's help available."

For the next half hour, Eli shared his own experiences and the strategies that had helped him cope with anxiety. The young man, whose name was Alex, listened intently, relief evident in his expression.

"Thank you," Alex said as their conversation wound down. "I've been trying to explain this to people for months, but you're the first person who seems to really get it."

Eli smiled. "Sometimes all it takes is someone who's been there. And hey, if you ever need to talk, I'm usually here working in the afternoons."

As Alex left, visibly more relaxed than when he'd arrived, Eli caught Sophie's eye from behind the counter. She gave him a knowing smile and a thumbs up.

In the months that followed, Eli found himself becoming something of an unofficial counselor at the coffee shop. Word spread about the empathetic regular who was always willing to lend an ear, and people began to seek him out.

He listened to a college student stressed about choosing a major, offering perspective without judgment. He comforted a grieving widow, sharing memories of his own loss and the healing power of time. He even mediated a dispute between two longtime friends, helping them see each other's points of view.

With each interaction, Eli felt more connected to his community. The empathy he showed others began to ripple outward, creating an atmosphere of understanding and support that permeated the entire coffee shop.

One day, as Eli settled into his usual spot, Sophie approached with his coffee and a mischievous grin.

"So," she said, sliding into the seat across from him. "When are you going to quit your day job and become our full-time therapist?"

Eli chuckled. "I don't know about that. I'm not a professional—I try to listen and understand."

Sophie shook her head. "You do more than that, Eli. You show people they're not alone. Do you have any idea how much of a difference you've made around here?"

Eli glanced around the bustling coffee shop. He saw Alex chatting animatedly with a coworker, looking more confident than ever. The college student he'd advised was explaining a complex topic to a study group, her earlier uncertainty replaced by enthusiasm. Even the once-feuding friends were sharing a table, laughing over some private joke.

"I guess I've had some good conversations," Eli admitted.

"It's more than that," Sophie insisted. "You've created a ripple effect. People who've talked to you go on to be more understanding with others. It's like you've taught this whole place the value of empathy."

Eli felt a warmth spread through his chest. "I'm just trying to be the person I needed when I was struggling," he said softly.

Sophie reached across the table and squeezed his hand. "Well, you're doing a pretty amazing job of it."

As Eli looked around the coffee shop—now more a community center than a mere business—he marveled at the power of empathy. What had started as a simple act of kindness on a difficult day had grown into something beautiful and transformative.

He thought back to that first conversation with Sophie when they were both weighed down by their personal struggles - how different things might have been if he'd taken his coffee and left.

As Eli reflected on the changes in the coffee shop, he realized that his own life had transformed as well. The once-isolated and stressed professional had become an integral part of a vibrant community. His empathetic nature, which he had often downplayed in his corporate job, was now his greatest strength.

One afternoon, as Eli was engrossed in his work, he noticed a new face enter the coffee shop. An elderly man, looking lost and a bit overwhelmed, approached the counter. Sophie greeted him warmly, but the man seemed flustered.

"I... I'm not sure what I want," the man mumbled, his eyes darting nervously around the menu board.

Eli watched as Sophie patiently explained the different options, her voice gentle and reassuring. It was a stark contrast to the frazzled barista he'd first met months ago. Eli smiled, realizing how much Sophie had grown in her own capacity for empathy.

As the elderly man made his way to a table, still looking a bit unsure, Eli caught his eye and offered a friendly nod. The man hesitated, then shuffled over to Eli's table.

"Mind if I join you?" the man asked, his voice quavering slightly. "I'm new to the neighborhood, and... well, I don't know anyone yet."

"Of course," Eli replied, gesturing to the empty chair. "I'm Eli. Welcome to the neighborhood."

The man introduced himself as Harold and began to share his story. He had recently moved to the area to be closer to his daughter after his wife passed away. The transition had been difficult, leaving him feeling isolated and out of place.

As Eli listened, he felt a familiar surge of empathy. He remembered his own feelings of loneliness when he first moved to the city for work. Gently, he began to share some of his experiences and the ways he had connected with the community.

"You know," Eli said, "this coffee shop has become a bit of a gathering place. There's a book club that meets here on Thursdays and a group of retirees who play chess on Sunday afternoons. You might enjoy joining them."

Harold's eyes lit up. "Really? I used to love chess, but I haven't played in years."

As they continued to talk, Eli noticed Harold becoming more animated. The nervousness that had clouded his features began to dissipate, replaced by a tentative hope.

Before long, Sophie approached their table with a smile. "Sorry to interrupt, but I couldn't help overhear about the chess group. Harold, if you're interested, I can introduce you to some of the regulars. They're always looking for new players."

Harold beamed. "That would be wonderful, thank you."

As Sophie led Harold over to a group of older gentlemen in the corner, Eli felt a sense of satisfaction. He had witnessed firsthand how a simple act of empathy—taking the time to listen and understand—could make a profound difference in someone's life.

Over the next few weeks, Eli watched as Harold became a regular fixture in the coffee shop. The once-lonely newcomer was now engaged in lively chess matches and animated conversations. He had found his place in the community, all because someone had taken the time to understand and welcome him.

Eli's reputation as a compassionate listener continued to grow. People from all walks of life sought him out for advice, comfort, or simply a non-judgmental ear. He listened to teenagers struggling with peer pressure, young parents overwhelmed by the demands of raising children, and middle-aged adults caring for aging parents.

Through it all, Eli remained humble, always insisting that he was doing what anyone would do. But those around him knew better. They saw the unique gift he had for making people feel heard and understood.

One day, as Eli was packing up to leave, a young woman approached him hesitantly. He recognized her as a frequent customer but had never spoken to her directly.

"Excuse me," she said softly. "Are you Eli? The one everyone talks to?"

Eli nodded, offering a warm smile. "That's me. How can I help?"

The woman took a deep breath. "I've been coming here for weeks, working up the courage to talk to you. I... I'm dealing with depression, and I don't know what to do."

Eli's heart went out to her. He could see the pain and fear in her eyes, emotions he was all too familiar with from his own battles with mental health.

"First of all," he said gently, "thank you for having the courage to speak up. That's often the hardest part."

For the next hour, Eli listened as the woman, Sarah, poured out her struggles. He shared his own experiences with depression, the strategies that had helped him, and the importance of seeking professional help.

By the end of their conversation, Sarah looked lighter, as if a great weight had been lifted from her shoulders. "Thank you," she whispered. "I don't feel so alone anymore."

As Sarah left with a promise to look into therapy options, Eli felt a mix of emotions. He was glad he could help, but he also recognized the enormous responsibility that came with being a confidant for so many people.

That night, as Eli lay in bed reflecting on the day, he realized that his life had taken an unexpected but deeply fulfilling turn. What had started as a simple act of kindness in a coffee shop had blossomed into a calling?

He thought about all the lives he had touched and all the people who had touched his life in return. The empathy he had shown had created a ripple effect, fostering a community of understanding and support.

Eli drifted off to sleep with a smile on his face, grateful for the power of empathy and the unexpected journey it had taken him on. He looked forward to what tomorrow might bring and the new connections he would make, one conversation at a time.

Empathy is the cornerstone of meaningful human connection. While active listening is a crucial skill in communication, it can become a hollow exercise if not rooted in genuine empathy. To truly grow and deepen our connections with others, we must approach each interaction with a sincere desire to understand and validate the experiences and emotions of those we engage with.

Imagine a world where everyone listened actively but without empathy. Conversations would be mechanical, devoid of the warmth and understanding that make human interactions so valuable. People might hear the words being spoken, but they would miss the underlying emotions, the unspoken fears, and the subtle nuances that give depth to our communications.

To illustrate this point, let's consider two scenarios:

Scenario 1: Active Listening Without Empathy

John approaches his colleague, Sarah, who is visibly upset about a project that went awry. He starts explaining the situation, his voice trembling slightly.

Sarah nods along, maintaining eye contact and occasionally saying "Uh-huh" or "I see." She's using all the right active listening techniques she learned in a recent workshop. However, her mind is already racing to solutions or judgments about John's competence. She's not truly trying to understand how John feels or why this situation is so upsetting to him.

At the end of the conversation, John feels like he's been heard in a technical sense but not understood on a deeper level. The interaction leaves him feeling somewhat hollow and disconnected.

Scenario 2: Active Listening with Empathy

Now, let's reimagine the same situation but with empathy at the core of the interaction.

As John approaches Sarah, she immediately notices his distress. She sets aside her current task and gives him her full attention, not just with her ears but with her heart.

As John explains the situation, Sarah listens intently, trying to put herself in his shoes. She considers how she might feel in a similar situation, but she's careful not to project her own emotions onto John.

When John finishes speaking, Sarah takes a moment before responding. "John, it sounds like this project meant a lot to you, and its failure has really shaken your confidence. Am I understanding that correctly?"

John nods, feeling a wave of relief that someone truly gets it.

Sarah continues, "I can only imagine how frustrating and disappointing that must be. You put so much effort into this project. It's completely understandable that you're upset."

In this scenario, John walks away feeling truly heard and understood. The empathy Sarah displayed has strengthened their connection and made John feel supported in a meaningful way.

Now, let's delve deeper into the elements that make empathetic listening so powerful and how we can cultivate this skill to grow our connections.

Things to Do:

1. Actively listen to understand the other person's point of view: Active listening is more than just hearing words; it's about absorbing the full message being conveyed, including the emotional undertones and unspoken elements. When we listen with empathy, we're like sailors charting the depths of an ocean, exploring the hidden contours of someone's thoughts and feelings.

To do this effectively:

- Give your full attention. Put away distractions like your phone or computer.
- Observe body language and tone of voice, which often communicate more than words alone.
- Resist the urge to formulate your response while the other person is still speaking.
- Try to understand not just what is being said but why it matters to the speaker.

For example, if a friend is telling you about a conflict with their partner, don't just focus on the facts of the argument. Try to understand the emotions behind it - the hurt, the fear, or the frustration they might be feeling.

2. Verbalize your efforts to see things from their perspective: After listening intently, it's crucial to articulate what you've understood. This shows that you're not just passively absorbing information but actively working to comprehend their experience.

You might say something like:

"It sounds like you felt betrayed when your colleague took credit for your idea. I can imagine how that would make you question your place in the team and perhaps even your career choices. Is that close to how you're feeling?"

This verbalization serves multiple purposes:

- It demonstrates that you've been listening attentively.
- It shows that you're making a genuine effort to understand their perspective.
- It gives the speaker an opportunity to clarify or expand on their feelings if they've misunderstood something.

3. Express validation and acknowledgment of their feelings: One of the most powerful aspects of empathy is the validation it provides. When we acknowledge someone's feelings as valid and understandable, we're offering them acceptance and support.

You might say:

"Given everything you've told me, it's completely natural that you'd feel angry and hurt. Anyone in your situation would likely have similar feelings."

This validation is crucial because it helps the person feel seen and understood. It can be incredibly comforting to know that another person considers your emotional response reasonable.

4. Ask thoughtful questions to deepen your understanding: Empathetic listening often involves gently probing to gain a fuller picture. These questions should come from a place of genuine curiosity and desire to understand, not from a need to satisfy your own curiosity or gather gossip.

Some examples of thoughtful questions:
-   "Can you tell me more about how that experience affected you?"
-   "What do you think was the most challenging part of that situation for you?"
-   "How has this changed your perspective on [relevant topic]?"

These questions show your genuine interest in understanding their perspective more deeply and can help the speaker explore their own feelings more thoroughly.

Things Not to Do:

1. Don't make assumptions about experiences or emotions: Even if you've been in a similar situation, avoid projecting your own experiences onto the other person. Everyone's context and emotional responses are unique.

Instead of saying, "Oh, I know exactly how you feel. When that happened to me, I was devastated," try something like, "That sounds really challenging. Could you help me understand more about how it affected you?"

This approach acknowledges the uniqueness of their experience and invites them to share more rather than assuming you already know how they feel.

2. Avoid dismissing or diminishing concerns: Comments like "It's not that bad" or "You'll get over it" can make the other person feel invalidated, even if you're trying to be helpful or optimistic.

Remember that their feelings are real and significant to them, even if the situation might not seem severe from an outside perspective. Instead of minimizing their concerns, try to understand why the situation feels so impactful to them.

3. Don't shift the focus back to yourself or your own agenda: While it can be tempting to share your own similar experiences, be cautious about how and when you do this. The focus should remain on the other person's experience and emotions.

If you do share a personal anecdote, make sure it's in service of showing understanding, not overshadowing their story. You might say, "I had a somewhat similar experience once, and I remember feeling very confused and hurt. Is that anything like what you're experiencing?"

Things to Look Out For:

1. Be aware of your own biases or preconceptions that may cloud your empathy

We all have biases that can interfere with our ability to empathize. Maybe you have a preconceived notion about a certain type of person or situation. Recognize when these biases arise and consciously set them aside to listen with an open mind.

For example, if a coworker is complaining about their workload, you might have a bias that they're just lazy or inefficient. Try to set that aside and truly listen to their perspective. There might be factors you're unaware of that are contributing to their struggle.

2. Notice when you feel tempted to problem-solve rather than truly empathize

It's a common impulse to want to fix things for others, but sometimes, people need to be heard and understood. If you find yourself jumping to solutions, take a step back and focus on understanding and validating their feelings first.

You can always ask, "Are you looking for suggestions, or do you just need someone to listen right now?" This gives the person the opportunity to guide the conversation in the direction they need.

3. Pay attention to nonverbal cues that indicate the other person feels heard and understood

Watch for signs of relief, relaxation, or openness in their body language. If they seem to be opening up more or showing appreciation for your listening, you're likely on the right track with your empathetic approach.

Some positive signs to look for:

- Relaxed posture
- Increased eye contact
- Deeper, more personal sharing
- Verbal expressions of feeling understood or relieved

The Power of Empathetic Listening in Action

Let's consider a more complex scenario to illustrate how these principles can play out in a real-life situation:

Maria, a team leader in a tech company, notices that one of her team members, Alex, has been underperforming lately. Instead of immediately reprimanding Alex or putting him on a performance improvement plan, Maria decides to approach the situation with empathy.

Maria invites Alex to a quiet meeting room, ensuring they have privacy and won't be interrupted. She begins the conversation with an open-ended question: "Alex, I've noticed some changes in your work lately. Can you tell me how things have been going for you?"

Alex hesitates at first, but seeing Maria's genuine concern, he begins to open up. He explains that his mother has been diagnosed with a serious illness, and he's been struggling to balance his work responsibilities with his new role as her primary caregiver.

As Alex speaks, Maria practices active, empathetic listening:

1. She gives Alex her full attention, maintaining eye contact and nodding to show she's engaged.

2. She observes Alex's body language, noticing his slumped shoulders and the worry lines on his forehead.
3. Maria resists the urge to offer solutions immediately or to share her own experiences with family illness. Instead, she focuses entirely on understanding Alex's situation.

After Alex finishes speaking, Maria takes a moment to process what she's heard before responding. She then verbalizes her understanding:

"Alex, it sounds like you're dealing with an incredibly challenging situation. You're trying to be there for your mother during her illness while also maintaining your work responsibilities. It must be overwhelming to feel pulled in these two important directions."

Alex nods, his eyes showing a mix of relief and emotion at being understood.

Maria continues, "I can only imagine how stressful and emotionally draining this must be for you. It's completely understandable that your work has been affected. You're dealing with something that would be difficult for anyone."

This validation visibly relaxes Alex. His shoulders are slightly lower, and he lets out a small sigh.

To deepen her understanding, Maria asks some thoughtful questions:

"Can you tell me more about how this situation has been affecting your day-to-day work? Are there specific tasks or responsibilities that have become particularly challenging?"

Alex explains that he's been having trouble focusing during the day due to a lack of sleep and worry. He's also had to take several unexpected days off for his mother's appointments, which has caused him to fall behind on projects.

Maria listened carefully and then asked, "What do you think would be most helpful for you in managing your work responsibilities during this time?"

This question shows Alex that Maria is not just listening passively but is actively seeking ways to support him. It also empowers Alex by involving him in finding solutions.

Throughout the conversation, Maria is careful to avoid common pitfalls:

1. She doesn't make assumptions about Alex's experience or emotions, even though she had a similar experience with her own father's illness a few years ago.
2. She doesn't diminish Alex's concerns by saying things like "These things happen" or "It's just a temporary setback."
3. She keeps the focus on Alex, resisting the temptation to share her own story unless Alex specifically asks for it.

As they continue talking, Maria notices positive changes in Alex's demeanor. His posture becomes more open, he makes more eye contact, and he begins to speak more freely about both his challenges and his ideas for managing them.

By the end of the conversation, they've worked together to create a temporary plan that will allow Alex to manage his work responsibilities while also caring for his mother. This includes some flexibility in his work hours, redistributing some of his tasks to other team members, and setting up regular check-ins with Maria.

More importantly, Alex leaves the meeting feeling understood, supported, and valued as both an employee and a human being. The empathy Maria displayed has strengthened their working relationship and increased Alex's loyalty to both Maria and the company.

This scenario demonstrates how empathetic listening can transform a potentially confrontational situation into an opportunity for understanding and problem-solving. By approaching the conversation with genuine empathy, Maria was able to:

1. Uncover the root cause of Alex's performance issues
2. Provide emotional support during a difficult time
3. Collaboratively develop solutions that work for both Alex and the company
4. Strengthen their professional relationship
5. Likely improve Alex's job satisfaction and loyalty

In the long run, this empathetic approach is likely to lead to better outcomes for everyone involved. Alex feels supported and is more likely to regain his previous level of performance once his personal situation stabilizes. The team benefits from improved communication and a culture of understanding. Maria has also demonstrated effective leadership by addressing performance issues while showing care for her team members' well-being.

This example illustrates how empathetic listening, when practiced authentically, can be a powerful tool for building stronger, more resilient connections in both personal and professional contexts. It shows that taking the time to understand and validate someone's experiences and emotions truly can lead to more effective problem-solving and stronger relationships.

Chapter 11: Be Patient and Present

"Like a skilled sailor weathering the waves, be patient and present - let the conversation ebb and flow at its own natural pace."

The soft chime of the coffee shop door drew Eli's attention as Jack walked in, fifteen minutes late as usual. Eli took a deep breath, reminding himself to stay patient and present. This was their weekly catch-up, a tradition they'd kept for years despite Jack's chronic tardiness.

"Hey, sorry I'm late," Jack said breathlessly as he slid into the chair across from Eli. His curly hair was disheveled, and his cheeks flushed from rushing.

Eli smiled, pushing down the slight annoyance he felt. "No worries. I'm glad you made it." He gestured to the extra coffee he'd ordered. "I got your usual."

Gratitude flashed across Jack's face as he took a long sip. "You're the best. Work has been crazy this week."

Eli nodded, settling in to listen. Jack had a tendency to ramble, his thoughts jumping from one topic to the next. It could be exhausting to follow at times, but Eli reminded himself to stay focused and attentive. This time together was important for both of them.

"So there's this new project we're working on," Jack began, launching into a detailed explanation of his latest work challenge. Eli listened carefully, asking questions when appropriate to show he was engaged.

Jack's hands moved animatedly as he spoke, nearly knocking over his coffee at one point. Eli resisted the urge to interrupt and instead gently moved the mug to a safer spot on the table. Jack barely seemed to notice, caught up in his story.

As Jack continued, Eli's mind started to wander. He caught himself thinking about his own to-do list for the day and the errands he needed to run after their coffee date. With conscious effort, Eli redirected his focus back to Jack. His enthusiasm was endearing, even if Eli didn't always follow the technical details of his work.

"...and then the client said they wanted to change direction completely, can you believe it?" Jack was saying, shaking his head in disbelief.

"That must be so frustrating," Eli replied, trying to empathize. "How are you handling the change?"

Jack sighed, running a hand through his hair. "It's been tough. I've been putting in a lot of extra hours trying to rework everything."

Eli nodded sympathetically. "Make sure you're taking care of yourself too. Have you been sleeping enough?"

A flicker of guilt passed over Jack's face. "Probably not as much as I should be," he admitted.

They sat in comfortable silence for a moment as Jack took another sip of his coffee. Eli noticed the dark circles under his eyes and the slight slump of his shoulders. His heart went out to him, knowing how hard he pushed himself.

"Hey," Eli said gently. "Why don't we do something fun this weekend? Maybe go for a hike or check out that new art exhibit? It might be good for you to take a break from work."

Jack hesitated, clearly torn. "I don't know if I can spare the time..."

"Just think about it," Eli encouraged. "Even a few hours away from your desk could help you recharge."

Jack nodded slowly. "Yeah, maybe you're right. I'll see if I can move some things around."

The conversation shifted to lighter topics - a movie Jack had recently seen, a funny story about his neighbor's cat. Eli found himself relaxing, enjoying the easy back-and-forth of their friendship.

As they chatted, Eli noticed Jack checking his phone with increasing frequency. His responses became more distracted, his eyes darting to the screen every few minutes. Eli felt a twinge of irritation but pushed it aside. Instead, he took a deep breath and recommitted to being fully present in the moment.

"Is everything okay?" Eli asked when Jack's gaze lingered on his phone a bit longer than usual.

Jack looked up, a hint of guilt in his expression. "Sorry, yeah. I just got an email from my boss about that project. I should probably head back to the office soon."

Eli nodded, tamping down his disappointment. Their time together always seemed to fly by so quickly. "Of course, I understand. Is there anything I can do to help?"

Jack shook his head, but Eli saw gratitude in his eyes. "Just talking it through with you has helped a lot. Thanks for listening."

"Anytime," Eli replied sincerely. "That's what friends are for."

As Jack gathered his things to leave, Eli made a conscious effort to savor these last few moments together. He took in the warmth of the coffee shop, the familiar cadence of Jack's voice, the comfort of their friendship.

"Same time next week?" Jack asked as he stood to go.

"Wouldn't miss it," Eli assured him with a smile.

After Jack left, Eli lingered at the table for a few minutes, reflecting on their conversation. Maintaining patience and presence wasn't always easy, especially with someone as scattered as Jack could be. But Eli knew the effort was worthwhile.

Their friendship had weathered many changes over the years - new jobs, moves, relationships. Through it all, these weekly coffee dates had remained a constant. They weren't always convenient, and sometimes they left Eli feeling drained. But they were also a source of connection, support, and understanding that Eli deeply valued.

As Eli finally gathered his own belongings to leave, he felt a sense of peace. Despite the challenges, he was grateful for the opportunity to practice patience and presence with Jack. It was a skill that benefited not just their friendship but all areas of Eli's life.

Walking out into the crisp afternoon air, Eli made a mental note to follow up with Jack later about potential weekend plans. Even if he couldn't make it, Eli wanted him to know he was thinking of him. Sometimes, being a good friend meant simply being there - patient, present, and ready to listen.

The rest of Eli's day felt lighter somehow, buoyed by the genuine connection he'd shared. It was a reminder of the power of truly showing up for the people in our lives, even when it's not always easy.

As Eli went about his errands, he became more attuned to the world around him. The vibrant colors of the flowers at the market, the laughter of children in the park, the smile of the cashier at the grocery store - all seemed a bit brighter, a bit more vivid.

Eli realized that the patience and presence he'd practiced with Jack was spilling over into other areas of his life. He felt more grounded, more aware, more appreciative of the small moments that make up a day.

That evening, as Eli prepared dinner, his phone buzzed with a text from Jack:

"Thanks again for listening today. You were right about needing a break - I'm in for that hike this weekend if you're still up for it."

Eli smiled, feeling a warm glow of satisfaction. Being patient and present sometimes meant planting seeds that took time to grow. But when they did, the results could be beautiful.

As Eli typed out a reply, he felt a renewed commitment to cultivating these qualities in all his relationships. It wasn't always easy, and Eli knew he'd have plenty more opportunities to practice. But the rewards - deeper connections, more meaningful interactions, a richer experience of life - were more than worth the effort.

The next time Jack was late for coffee or distracted by work, Eli knew he'd be better equipped to handle it with grace and understanding. And in doing so, he'd be a better friend to Jack and a better version of himself.

In a world that often feels rushed and disconnected, choosing to be patient and present is a radical act of love - for others and for ourselves. It's a choice we can make every day, in every interaction, no matter how small.

The importance of patience cannot be overstated. It is the foundation upon which true connection and understanding are built. When we approach others with patience, we create an environment of trust, empathy, and openness.

Giving someone your full attention, allowing the conversation to flow naturally, and practicing patience show that you value their time and presence. It creates a space for deeper connection, understanding, and growth. Even the most scattered or distracted person can feel heard and cared for when met with an attitude of openness and compassion.

The time we share with others may be fleeting, but the impact of our patience and presence can ripple out in profound ways. When we are fully present, we find ourselves more attuned to the beauty around us, more grounded in each moment. And we carry the warmth of those connections as a source of renewal, a reminder to slow down and savor the simple joys.

Patience is not always easy, especially in a world that prizes speed and efficiency. It requires us to let go of our agenda, suspend our judgments, and truly listen. But the rewards of this practice are immeasurable.

Things to Do:

1. Give the person your undivided attention, "anchoring your focus like a ship moored in the harbor." When engaging in a conversation, giving the other person your complete and undivided attention is crucial. Imagine your focus as a ship securely anchored in a harbor. Just as a well-moored ship remains steady despite the surrounding waves and currents, your attention should stay fixed on the person speaking, unmoved by external distractions or internal thoughts.

This level of focus requires conscious effort. Begin by positioning yourself to face the speaker directly, maintaining comfortable eye contact. Let your gaze rest on their face, showing that you're fully present and engaged. Avoid fidgeting or engaging in nervous habits that might suggest your mind is elsewhere.

As you listen, actively process their words. Don't simply wait for your turn to speak, but truly absorb what they're saying. Visualize their words, empathize with their emotions, and try to understand their perspective. This deep level of attention helps you better comprehend their message and makes the speaker feel valued and heard.

Remember, your attention is one of the most precious gifts you can give someone. By anchoring your focus firmly on the conversation, you create a safe space for open, honest communication.

2. Allow the conversation to unfold at its own pace without rushing or trying to control the currents: Patience is key in any meaningful interaction. Just as you wouldn't try to force a river to flow faster, allow the conversation to progress at its natural pace. Resist the urge to rush through topics or push for quick resolutions. Instead, let the dialogue meander and explore various tributaries of thought.

This approach requires a certain level of surrender. You must let go of your own agenda and timeline, trusting that the conversation will reach its destination in due course. It's about being present in each moment rather than anxiously anticipating the next point or planning your response.

Allowing the conversation to unfold organically creates space for deeper insights and unexpected revelations. The other person may need time to articulate their thoughts or feelings fully. Giving them this time shows respect for their process and can lead to more authentic and meaningful exchanges.

3. Avoid interrupting or redirecting the topic prematurely: Interruptions are like sudden gusts of wind that can throw a conversation off course. Even if you're bursting with a relevant point or an exciting idea, hold back from interjecting. Wait for a natural pause or until the speaker has clearly finished their thought before contributing.

Sometimes, the urge to interrupt stems from a fear of forgetting what you want to say. If this is the case, try briefly noting down key words to remind yourself later. This allows you to stay present in the moment while ensuring you don't lose track of your own thoughts.

Similarly, resist the temptation to redirect the topic prematurely. The conversation may veer in a direction you didn't anticipate, but these detours often lead to valuable insights. Trust the natural flow of the dialogue, allowing topics to evolve organically rather than forcing the conversation back to a predetermined path.

4. Pace your responses to match the other person's tempo, "riding the rhythm of their words." Every person has their own conversational rhythm, like a unique melody. Some speak quickly, with rapid-fire thoughts and energetic gestures. Others are more deliberate, taking time to choose their words carefully. To truly connect, try to match the other person's pace and energy level.

If they speak slowly and thoughtfully, resist the urge to fill silences or rush them along. Instead, adopt a similar pace in your responses, allowing for comfortable pauses and measured replies. If they're more animated and quick-paced, you might slightly pick up your tempo to match their energy.

This synchronization, often called "mirroring," helps build rapport and makes the other person feel more comfortable. It's like finding the right dance partner – the interaction flows more smoothly when you're in step with each other.

Things Not to Do:

1. Don't multitask or let your mind wander during the interaction, "letting your attention drift like a rudderless boat." In our hyper-connected world, it's all too easy to fall into the trap of multitasking. However, dividing your attention is like letting your boat drift without direction. You may think you're making progress on multiple fronts, but in reality, you're not fully present in any single task.

During a conversation, commit to being fully there. Put away any work or personal tasks that might tempt you to split your focus. If you're meeting virtually, close unnecessary tabs or applications that might distract you. If intrusive thoughts about other responsibilities arise, gently acknowledge them and then return your focus to the present moment.

Remember, true listening is an active process. It requires your full mental and emotional engagement. When you give someone your undivided attention, you're not just hearing their words — you're picking up on subtle nuances in tone, observing body language, and connecting on a deeper level.

2. Avoid checking your phone, glancing at the clock, or exhibiting other distracting behaviors: The temptation to check our phones is almost reflexive in our digital age. However, glancing at your device during a conversation sends a clear message that something else is more important than the person in front of you. It's like dropping anchor in the middle of a journey — it disrupts the flow and momentum of the interaction.

Similarly, frequent clock-watching can make the other person feel rushed or unimportant. If time constraints are a concern, addressing this upfront rather than constantly checking the time during your conversation is better.

Other distracting behaviors to avoid include fidgeting excessively, looking around the room, or engaging in unrelated activities. These actions can make you appear disinterested or uncomfortable, potentially causing the other person to withdraw or lose confidence in the conversation.

3. Don't try to fill every silence with your own words, "disrupting the natural tides of the exchange." Silence in a conversation is not an enemy to be vanquished but a natural part of the ebb and flow of dialogue. Many people feel uncomfortable with pauses and rush to fill them with words, but this can disrupt the natural rhythm of the exchange.

Silence serves many purposes in conversation. It allows time for reflection, gives space for emotions to be processed, and can emphasize important points. By allowing comfortable silences, you're creating room for deeper thoughts to surface and for the other person to gather their thoughts.

Moreover, constantly filling silences with your own words can overwhelm the other person and turn the conversation into a monologue rather than a dialogue. Learn to be comfortable with pauses, viewing them as productive parts of the conversation rather than awkward gaps to be filled.

Things to Look Out For:

1. Be aware of your own impatience or discomfort with silence, "feeling the restless urge to set sail before the winds are right." Self-awareness is crucial in maintaining patience and presence. Pay attention to your own internal state during the conversation. Do you feel a sense of restlessness or urgency? Are you tempted to rush through topics or push for quick conclusions?

This impatience often manifests as physical sensations — perhaps a tightness in your chest, an urge to fidget, or a desire to interrupt. When you notice these feelings arising, take a deep breath and consciously recommit to being present. Remind yourself that meaningful conversations, like successful voyages, can't always be rushed.

If you find yourself consistently struggling with impatience in conversations, it might be helpful to explore the root causes. Are you often pressed for time? Do you have a habit of trying to control outcomes? Understanding these patterns can help you develop strategies to cultivate greater patience.

2. Notice when you feel the urge to "fix" or problem-solve rather than listen, "trying to chart a course instead of observing the currents." Many of us, especially those with nurturing or leadership tendencies, have a strong impulse to solve problems as soon as we hear about them. However, jumping straight into problem-solving mode can sometimes be counterproductive in a conversation.

When someone is sharing a challenge or difficulty, they often need to feel heard and understood before they're ready for solutions. By immediately offering advice or trying to fix the situation, you might inadvertently minimize their feelings or make them feel you're not listening.

Instead of charting a course out of their troubles, focus first on fully understanding the currents they're navigating. Ask clarifying questions, reflect back on what you've heard, and validate their emotions. Only once they feel truly heard should you consider offering advice – and even then, ask if they're open to suggestions rather than presuming they want your solutions.

3. Pay attention to nonverbal cues that indicate the other person feels heard and respected: Communication is about much more than just words. A significant portion of our message is conveyed through nonverbal cues – body language, facial expressions, tone of voice, and even the energy we project. As you practice being patient and present, develop your ability to read these subtle signals.

Watch for signs that the other person feels comfortable and heard. These might include relaxed body posture, maintained eye contact, and engaged facial expressions. This often indicates interest and connection if they're leaning slightly towards you. A genuine smile or nod can signal agreement or appreciation for your attentiveness.

Conversely, be alert for signs of discomfort or disengagement. If the person starts to fidget, frequently looks away, or crosses their arms tightly, they may be feeling unheard or defensive. Subtle changes in tone of voice or speaking pace can also provide valuable information about their emotional state.

You can adjust your approach in real-time by paying close attention to these nonverbal cues. If you sense discomfort, you might need to slow down, ask more questions, or reassure them that you're genuinely interested in what they're saying. You can build on that connection to deepen the conversation if you notice positive engagement.

Remember, being truly present means engaging with all aspects of communication, not just the spoken words. It's about creating a safe, respectful space where the other person feels valued and understood.

Chapter 12: Offer a Token of Kindness

If you feel comfortable and if it's appropriate, consider offering a small token of kindness to leave a lasting positive impression. This could be a compliment, a piece of advice, or even a small tangible gift. Like a message in a bottle found adrift in the sea, this unexpected gesture can turn a brief encounter into a memorable moment, reinforcing the positive connection you've made. Always ensure your offering is genuine, respectful, and appropriate for the situation and the person you're interacting with.

Eli made his way through the bustling train station, weaving between the throngs of hurried commuters. His eyes scanned the crowd, searching for an open seat where he could settle in for the long ride home.

As he turned the corner, a flash of movement caught his eye - a young woman sitting hunched over on a bench, her shoulders slumped and her expression downcast. Something about her tugged at Eli's heart, and he found himself instinctively drawn to her.

Approaching cautiously, Eli cleared his throat. "Excuse me, miss? Is this seat taken?"

The woman looked up, a flicker of surprise crossing her face. "Oh, no, no, please, have a seat," she said, shifting her bag to make room.

Eli sat down, offering her a gentle smile. Up close, he could see the telltale signs of distress - the redness around her eyes, the trembling of her hands as she fidgeted with the strap of her bag.

"I couldn't help but notice you look a bit...down," Eli said softly. "Is everything alright?"

The woman let out a heavy sigh, her gaze dropping to the floor. "I'm just...having a really bad day, that's all. Nothing seems to be going right."

Eli nodded sympathetically. "I'm sorry to hear that. We all have those days where everything feels like it's falling apart. Would you like to talk about it? Sometimes, it helps to get things off your chest."

For a moment, the woman hesitated. Then, as if a dam had burst, the words came spilling out. She told Eli about the argument she'd had with her boyfriend that morning, the frustrating technical issues she'd faced at work, and the stack of bills piling up on her kitchen table. With each revelation, her voice grew more strained, her eyes glistening with unshed tears.

Eli listened intently, offering the occasional nod or murmur of understanding. He knew all too well the feeling of being overwhelmed, of having one's problems compound until it felt as though the world was closing in. As the woman's story unfolded, his heart went out to her.

When she finally fell silent, Eli placed a gentle hand on her arm. "That sounds like an incredibly difficult day. I can only imagine how exhausting it must be to deal with all of that at once."

The woman wiped her eyes, offering Eli a watery smile. "I'm sorry; I don't know why I'm unloading all of this on a complete stranger. You must think I'm a mess."

"Not at all," Eli reassured her. "Sometimes it helps to have an impartial ear, someone who can just listen without judgment. And believe me, I've had my fair share of those kinds of days. You're not alone."

A flicker of gratitude crossed the woman's face, and Eli could sense a slight easing of the tension in her posture.

As the train halted to a stop, the woman got up, her fingers still fidgeting with the strap of her bag. "Thank you, truly," she said, offering Eli a watery smile.

With that, she made her way off the train, disappearing into the throng of commuters. Eli watched her go, a sense of peace settling over him. In that brief encounter, he had been able to offer a small glimmer of hope to a stranger in need – a simple act of kindness that had the power to uplift and inspire.

As Eli disembarked the train and made his way through the bustling station, his mind kept returning to the woman and her story. He couldn't shake the sense that there was more he could do to uplift her spirits, to ensure that his small gesture had a lasting impact.

Pausing at a small bakery, Eli purchased a fresh, warm donut, its aroma wafting through the air. With a determined stride, he retraced his steps, scanning the crowd for any sign of the woman.

Finally, he spotted her waiting on the platform, her gaze downcast as she clutched the strap of her bag. Approaching cautiously, Eli cleared his throat. "Excuse me, miss? I hope you don't mind, but I couldn't stop thinking about our conversation earlier."

The woman looked up, a flash of recognition crossing her features. "Oh, it's you. I...I'm so sorry; I didn't mean to unload all that on you."

Eli held up a hand, offering her a reassuring smile. "Please, don't apologize. I'm glad we had the chance to talk." Extending the donut toward her, he continued, "I wanted to offer you this. It's fresh from the bakery, and I thought you might enjoy a little pick-me-up after the day you've had."

The woman's eyes widened in surprise, a hesitant smile tugging at the corners of her mouth. "You really didn't have to do that," she murmured, accepting the pastry with a trembling hand.

"I know," Eli replied, "but I wanted to. Sometimes, when we're feeling our lowest, a small gesture of kindness can make all the difference."

As the woman took a bite of the donut, a look of pure delight crossed her features. "This is delicious," she said, her voice thick with emotion. "Thank you, truly. You've no idea how much this means to me."

Eli felt a swell of satisfaction, knowing that his actions had the power to uplift her spirits, even if just for a fleeting moment. "I'm glad you're enjoying it. And please, remember what I said – this too shall pass. Brighter days are ahead, I promise."

The woman nodded, her eyes glistening with unshed tears. "I won't forget this. Thank you for listening and for...for everything."

As the train pulled into the station, Eli gave her arm a gentle squeeze. "Take care of yourself. And if you ever need someone to talk to, feel free to reach out. I'll be here."

With a final nod, the woman boarded the train, the donut clutched tightly in her hand. Eli watched her go, a sense of purpose and connection washing over him. In that brief encounter, he had made a meaningful difference in a stranger's life – and that was a gift he would cherish.

As Eli made his way home, he couldn't help but feel a renewed sense of determination. In a world that often feels harsh and overwhelming, the simple act of offering a token of kindness – a word of encouragement, a gesture of support, a small tangible gift – had the power to transform lives, one interaction at a time.

It was a lesson he vowed to carry with him, a testament to the transformative power of empathy and the profound impact that a single act of compassion can have. As he walked through the door of his apartment, Eli couldn't help but feel a deep sense of gratitude – not just for the opportunity to uplift a stranger but for the reminder that even in our darkest hours, there are people out there who are willing to extend a hand, to offer a glimmer of light in the darkness.

As we've explored in the previous chapters, building meaningful connections with new people requires a delicate balance of open-ended questioning, active listening, and genuine engagement. By inviting others to share their stories and fully immersing ourselves in their perspectives, we lay the foundation for rewarding interactions that extend beyond a single encounter.

However, there is one additional element that can truly elevate a chance meeting into a memorable, lasting experience - the offering of a small token of kindness. This unexpected gesture, given with thoughtfulness and sincerity, can transform a fleeting interaction into something truly special, leaving a profound and positive impression on the recipient.

The Power of a Thoughtful Gesture

In our fast-paced, often impersonal world, small acts of kindness can feel like a rare and precious commodity. When we take the time to offer a genuine compliment, a heartfelt word of encouragement, or even a modest tangible gift, we communicate something powerful: "I see you. I value you. You matter."

These tokens of kindness do more than brighten someone's day in the moment. They can have a ripple effect, inspiring the recipient to pay that positivity forward and potentially creating an uplifting domino effect. Moreover, studies have shown that the act of giving itself can boost our own mood, fostering a greater sense of connection and well-being.

But beyond the individual benefits, offering tokens of kindness can also strengthen the bonds we form with new people. When we make an effort to go above and beyond the typical social script, we signal that this interaction holds a deeper meaning for us. We invite the other person to see us as thoughtful, caring individuals rather than just another passing acquaintance.

This unexpected gesture can be particularly impactful in the context of a chance encounter or a brief interaction. In these situations, where we may not have the opportunity for an extended dialogue, a token of kindness can leave a lasting positive impression and inspire the other person to reflect on our interaction long after it has ended.

Imagine, for instance, striking up a conversation with a stranger while waiting in line at the grocery store. After an engaging discussion about your shared interests or experiences, you could conclude the interaction by saying, "You know, I really enjoyed our chat. It's been a pleasure getting to know you a bit. Here, I want you to have this - I hope it brightens your day."

As you hand them a small, thoughtful gift, whether it's a piece of homemade baked goods, a book recommendation, or even just a sincere compliment, you communicate that this was no ordinary interaction. You've invested a piece of yourself, however modest, to make a genuine connection. The recipient is likely to remember that moment of warmth and kindness long after the initial conversation has faded.

Of course, it's important to exercise discretion and ensure that any token of kindness is appropriate for the situation and the individual. The goal is to leave a positive impression, not to make the other person uncomfortable or put them in an awkward position. But when offered with care and sensitivity, these small gestures can be incredibly powerful.

Choosing the Right Token of Kindness

So, what exactly constitutes an appropriate token of kindness? The options are vast and can be tailored to the specific person and context. The key is to choose something thoughtful, relevant, and given with a genuine, altruistic intention.

Verbal Tokens

Sometimes, the most meaningful tokens are those that don't require any material exchange. A sincere compliment, for example, can go a long way in brightening someone's day and reinforcing your positive impression of them.

When offering a verbal token, focus on specific, authentic observations that highlight the person's unique strengths, talents, or character. Avoid generic platitudes and instead speak from the heart. Perhaps you were struck by the person's infectious enthusiasm, their insightful perspective, or their kind demeanor. Articulating what you genuinely admire about them can be a powerful gift.

You might also consider sharing a word of encouragement or affirmation. If the person mentioned a challenge they were facing or a goal they were working toward, you could say something like, "I really admire your determination to [achieve that goal]. I have no doubt you'll get there - you've got this!" These uplifting messages can provide a much-needed boost of confidence and motivation.

Tangible Tokens

In addition to verbal tokens, you may also choose to offer a small tangible gift. The key here is to select something thoughtful, practical, and aligned with the person's interests or needs. Avoid anything that could be seen as overly extravagant or inappropriate.

For instance, if you bonded with someone over a shared love of reading, you could recommend a book you think they'd enjoy, perhaps even lending them your own copy. Or, if the person mentioned a hobby or passion, you could give them a small trinket or memento related to that interest.

The beauty of tangible tokens is that they serve as a physical reminder of your connection long after the initial encounter. The recipient can revisit the gift and be reminded of your thoughtfulness and the positive interaction you shared.

However, when choosing a tangible token, it's crucial to be mindful of cultural norms, personal boundaries, and power dynamics. Avoid anything that could be perceived as flirtatious, or that might make the recipient uncomfortable. The goal is to uplift them, not to make them feel obligated or pressured in any way.

Contextual Tokens

Sometimes, the most impactful tokens of kindness are those that are tailored to the specific situation or environment. These contextual gestures demonstrate your keen observation skills and your ability to respond to the needs of the moment.

For example, if you're chatting with someone while waiting in a long line, you could offer them a bottle of water or a snack to help them endure the wait. Or if you notice someone struggling to carry their belongings, you could lend a hand and assist them. These small acts of service not only brighten the person's day but also showcase your thoughtfulness and willingness to go the extra mile.

Contextual tokens can also involve sharing valuable information or resources. If the person mentions a challenge they're facing, you could provide a relevant recommendation, contact, or piece of advice that might help them. This level of care and consideration can be incredibly meaningful, as it demonstrates that you were truly listening and want to support them in a tangible way.

Regardless of the form it takes, the key to a successful token of kindness is to ensure that it is genuine, appropriate, and aligns with the person's needs and preferences. When offered with sincerity and compassion, these small gestures can have a profound and lasting impact, transforming a chance encounter into a memorable moment of human connection.

Overcoming Hesitation and Embracing Vulnerability

For many of us, the idea of offering a token of kindness to a stranger can feel daunting or even uncomfortable. We may worry about overstepping boundaries, making the other person feel awkward, or simply feeling self-conscious about our gestures.

These hesitations are understandable, as putting ourselves out there and making ourselves vulnerable can be a significant challenge. We may fear rejection, judgment, or simply the uncertainty of how our gesture will be received.

However, it's important to remember that the act of offering a token of kindness is inherently an act of courage and empathy. By going beyond the typical social script and extending a genuine, thoughtful gesture, we communicate that we see the other person as a fellow human worthy of our care and attention.

Moreover, research has shown that small acts of kindness, even from strangers, can have a profound impact on the recipient's mood, outlook, and sense of connection. Even if they initially feel surprised or unsure, the vast majority of people will appreciate the thoughtfulness and warmth behind your gesture.

So, how can we overcome our hesitation and embrace the vulnerability required to offer a token of kindness?

One of the key mindset shifts to make is recognizing that the act of offering a token of kindness is not about you but about the other person. It's easy to get caught up in worrying about how we'll be perceived or what the other person might think of us. But when we reframe it as an opportunity to brighten someone's day and potentially create a meaningful connection, it becomes a truly selfless act.

Approaching it with genuine care and compassion, rather than anxiety or self-consciousness, can make all the difference. Remind yourself that your sole intention is to positively impact the recipient, to let them know they matter and are seen. This shift in focus can help overcome the natural hesitation we often feel about putting ourselves out there.

It's also important to start small and build confidence gradually. Begin with something as simple as a sincere compliment or word of encouragement. These low-risk tokens allow you to test the waters and get comfortable with the vulnerability required without feeling like you're taking a huge leap.

As you gain experience, you can then expand to more substantial gestures, always making sure they align with the person's needs and preferences. The key is to trust your intuition - if you feel a genuine, altruistic urge to offer a token of kindness, chances are your instincts are picking up on something special about that individual and the potential for a meaningful exchange.

Of course, it's crucial to accept that you cannot control how the other person will respond. Some may enthusiastically receive your gesture, while others may react with surprise or even discomfort. Regardless, trust that your act of kindness has value in and of itself. Even if the recipient doesn't outwardly express their gratitude, your token has the power to uplift them, even if just for a fleeting moment.

Moreover, remember that by embracing the vulnerability required to offer a token of kindness, you are modeling a powerful example of empathy, compassion, and human connection.

It's important to note that while the overall intent should be selfless, offering tokens of kindness can also have personal benefits. Studies have shown that the act of giving can boost our own mood, foster a greater sense of well-being, and strengthen our social bonds. So, in a sense, these gestures are a win-win—they uplift both the giver and the receiver.

Ultimately, overcoming the hesitation to offer a token of kindness is about cultivating the courage to step outside our comfort zones and make ourselves vulnerable. It's about recognizing that the potential reward — the opportunity to brighten someone's day, to forge a meaningful connection, and to be a force for good in the world — far outweighs the temporary discomfort we might feel.

So, the next time you find yourself in a chance encounter with a stranger, I encourage you to listen to that intuitive nudge prompting you to extend a token of kindness.

Chapter 13: Conclusion

In an increasingly disconnected world, where screens and devices often take precedence over face-to-face interaction, the ability to forge genuine, lasting connections with others has become more vital than ever before. As Eli's story so powerfully illustrated, even a single chance encounter, guided by the principles of empathy and compassion, has the power to transform lives - both the lives of those we reach out to and our own.

Now, more than ever, we must reclaim the art of human connection. Yet, it is precisely in these moments of vulnerability that we unlock the greatest opportunities for growth, understanding, and profound fulfillment.

By embracing this transformative journey and putting the eleven key principles of effective human interaction into practice, you too can cultivate meaningful connections that enrich not only the lives of those you meet but your own life as well.

In a world that can sometimes feel cold and isolating, the power of these principles to spark hope, empathy, and a renewed sense of our shared humanity cannot be overstated. By stepping outside our comfort zones and embracing the vulnerability required to connect with strangers, we open ourselves up to unexpected revelations, profound growth, and the immense joy that arises from the profound experience of being truly seen and understood.

So, let us embark on this journey together, fueled by a renewed commitment to forging the kinds of connections that can transform not only individual lives but the very fabric of our communities.

Principle 1: Radiate Positive Energy

How you approach an interaction can set that encounter's entire tone and trajectory. By radiating a warm, confident, and optimistic energy, you have the power to instantly put others at ease and create an inviting environment for connection.

Start by paying attention to your body language - stand tall, make eye contact, and greet people with a genuine smile. Your facial expressions and gestures communicate volumes about your state of mind and your openness to engage. Exude an aura of self-assurance and positivity, and you'll find that people are naturally drawn to you.

But positive energy goes beyond just your physical presence. It's also about the attitude and mindset you bring to each interaction. Approach every new person you meet with a spirit of openness, curiosity, and goodwill. Rather than making assumptions or judgments, seek to understand their unique perspective and lived experiences.

This doesn't mean being inauthentic or putting on a performance. Quite the opposite, in fact. By tapping into your own inherent sense of self-worth and optimism, you'll radiate an energy that is both compelling and disarming. People will sense your sincerity and be more inclined to let their guard down and engage with you in a meaningful way.

Principle 2: Nerves Are Normal

Even the most seasoned communicators can feel a flutter of nerves when entering unfamiliar social situations. That surge of adrenaline, the racing heart, the sweaty palms - these physiological responses are a completely natural part of the human experience.

Our brains are hardwired to be highly attuned to social cues and the potential for acceptance or rejection. Whenever we encounter a new person or environment where our sense of belonging feels threatened, our fight-or-flight response kicks in. It's an evolutionary adaptation that served our ancestors well, preparing them to handle physical threats to their safety.

However, that same biological reaction can manifest in the modern world even in relatively low-stakes social interactions. Your brain doesn't always distinguish between life-or-death danger and the simple act of introducing yourself to a new acquaintance. So those familiar butterflies often flutter to life when we're putting ourselves out there, whether it's at a networking event, a party, or a job interview.

The key is to recognize that these feelings of anxiety are normal, not a sign of weakness or inadequacy. They don't mean you're incapable or unworthy - they mean you're human. Accepting this truth is the first step toward harnessing your nerves instead of letting them control you.

Rather than berating yourself for feeling nervous, try reframing those sensations as a natural, healthy response. Silently thank your body for providing you with the extra energy and heightened senses to handle the situation with grace.

Breathe into the discomfort, allowing it to fuel your interactions rather than derail them.

When you shift your mindset this way, you start to see nerves not as an obstacle but as an ally. That adrenaline surge can work in your favor, heightening your focus, boosting your performance, and imbuing your interactions with a palpable sense of excitement and anticipation.

Of course, that's not to say you should ignore your nerves or pretend they don't exist. Trying to suppress or deny those feelings is a surefire way to heighten their intensity. The goal isn't to eliminate nerves entirely but rather to develop strategies for managing them effectively.

Breathing exercises, positive self-talk, and visualization techniques can all be powerful tools in your arsenal. Confiding with trusted friends about your anxiety can also provide a sense of support and perspective. The more you practice acknowledging and navigating your nerves, the more adept you'll become at harnessing that energy productively.

Ultimately, the ability to recognize and accept your nerves as a normal part of the human experience is a key ingredient in mastering the art of effective communication. By embracing the vulnerability required to step outside your comfort zone, you open yourself up to opportunities for profound growth, connection, and fulfillment.

Principle 3: Respect Personal Boundaries

As you strive to connect with new people, it's crucial to remain attuned to their personal boundaries and comfort levels.

Respecting individuals' space and privacy is essential for building trust and rapport.

Pay close attention to nonverbal cues - body language, tone of voice, eye contact, and responsiveness. These subtle signals can tell you a lot about how someone is feeling in the moment and whether they're open to deeper engagement. If you notice someone seeming guarded or withdrawn, take a step back and adjust your approach accordingly.

It's also important to be mindful of physical proximity. Don't invade someone's personal space unless you have a clear indication that they're comfortable with it. Start with a friendly yet appropriate distance, and allow the other person to determine the pace of any physical interaction, whether a handshake, a pat on the shoulder, or a hug.

Respecting boundaries doesn't mean you can't be warm and personable. In fact, by demonstrating that you recognize and respect someone's need for autonomy, you're creating conditions for them to feel safe opening up to you. It's all about finding the right balance between engagement and deference.

Principle 4: Deliver a Warm Greeting

The importance of a warm greeting cannot be overstated in the realm of human connection. It serves as the gateway to meaningful interaction and sets the tone for the entire encounter. A thoughtful, genuine greeting has the power to transform a mundane exchange into a memorable connection.

First impressions are formed within seconds of meeting someone, and your initial greeting plays a crucial role in shaping that impression. A warm, welcoming approach can instantly disarm barriers and create an atmosphere of trust and openness. This is particularly vital in today's fast-paced, often impersonal world, where genuine human connections are increasingly rare and valuable.

A warm greeting signals respect and acknowledgment of the other person's presence and inherent worth. It communicates that you see them not just as another face in the crowd but as an individual worthy of your time and attention. This simple act of recognition can be profoundly impactful, especially for those who may feel invisible or overlooked in their daily lives.

Moreover, the energy and intention behind your greeting can significantly influence the trajectory of the interaction. A warm, sincere welcome creates a positive emotional context, making the other person more likely to respond in kind. This reciprocal exchange of positivity can lead to more open, productive, and enjoyable conversations.

From a psychological perspective, a warm greeting activates the brain's reward centers, releasing feel-good neurotransmitters like dopamine and serotonin. This makes the interaction more pleasant for both parties and enhances the likelihood of forming a lasting positive association between you and the encounter.

A warm greeting can be a powerful tool for building rapport and establishing productive relationships in professional settings. It sets a tone of collegiality and respect, which can facilitate smoother collaborations and negotiations.

For those in service-oriented roles, mastering the art of the warm greeting is essential. It can significantly enhance customer satisfaction, loyalty, and overall experience, directly impacting business success.

On a broader societal level, warm greetings contribute to a culture of kindness and connection. In a world often characterized by division and indifference, these small acts of warmth and acknowledgment can ripple outward, fostering a more empathetic and connected community.

Principle 5: Be Genuine and Authentic

Being true to yourself when meeting new people sets the foundation for honest relationships and creates an environment where others feel safe to be themselves.

The importance of authenticity in forging new connections cannot be overstated. When you present your true self, flaws and all, you invite others to do the same. This mutual vulnerability becomes the bedrock upon which deep, lasting relationships are built. Through this genuine exchange, people can truly see and understand each other, moving beyond surface-level pleasantries to form real bonds.

Authenticity breeds trust, a crucial element in any relationship. When people sense you're being genuine, they're more likely to let their guard down and open up to you. This trust allows for more honest, open communication, which is essential for building strong connections. In contrast, when people detect inauthenticity, it can create a barrier to trust and hinder the development of a meaningful relationship.

Being genuine also makes you more relatable. Everyone has insecurities, quirks, and challenges. By embracing and sharing yours, you create points of connection with others who may be experiencing similar things. This shared humanity can be a powerful force in bringing people together, as it reminds us that we're not alone in our experiences.

Moreover, authenticity allows your unique qualities to shine through. In a world where many people try to fit into predetermined molds, your genuine self stands out. This distinctiveness can be attractive to others, drawing them to your unique perspective and experiences. It's often these authentic traits that people remember and appreciate most about you.

Authenticity also conserves mental and emotional energy. Trying to be someone you're not is exhausting and unsustainable. By being genuine, you free up that energy to be present in your interactions, listen more attentively, and engage more fully with the people you meet.

In professional settings, authenticity can be a valuable asset. It fosters trust with colleagues and clients, enhances your credibility, and can lead to more productive collaborations. Authentic leaders are often more respected and effective, as their genuineness inspires loyalty and open communication within their teams.

Being authentic also allows for more meaningful personal growth. When you're true to yourself, you can more accurately assess your strengths and areas for improvement. This self-awareness is crucial for personal development and can lead to more fulfilling relationships as you continue to grow and evolve.

It's important to note that being authentic doesn't mean sharing every thought or feeling indiscriminately. Rather, it's about being true to your values, expressing yourself honestly, and allowing your genuine personality to come through in your interactions.

Principle 6: Mastering the Art of Asking Questions

Building authentic relationships hinges on one simple yet often overlooked skill: asking meaningful, open-ended questions. While questions are commonly viewed as a tool for gathering information, they can also be a doorway to connection and understanding. Asking the right questions creates opportunities to truly connect with others, build trust, and know people on a deeper, more personal level. Mastering this skill can reveal unique perspectives, stories, and emotions that shape who people are, unlocking richer relationships and fostering profound personal growth.

At its core, human connection is about being seen, heard, and understood. When you engage someone with a genuine question, you're not just seeking facts; you're inviting them to share their inner world, their values, and their viewpoints. This goes beyond small talk—it's the foundation for meaningful bonds. By asking questions with intention and curiosity, you give the other person space to open up, share their thoughts, and reveal the layers that make them who they are. Open-ended questions, specifically, encourage dialogue rather than yes-or-no answers, creating a safe space for authenticity and deeper mutual understanding.

One of the most powerful aspects of asking thoughtful questions is the impact it has on both the asker and the person answering. For the person responding, such questions offer a chance to feel validated and valued. When someone asks you about your feelings, experiences, or beliefs, it's a message that they care about your perspective. This acknowledgment can strengthen the bond, building trust and openness essential for genuine connections.

On the flip side, the act of asking questions benefits the asker just as much. By being curious about another person, you invite yourself into their world, stepping outside your own experiences and gaining insights into someone else's. The more you learn about others, the more you begin to see the world through different lenses, enriching your perspective and deepening your empathy.

Mastering the art of open-ended questioning strengthens relationships by fostering rapport and intimacy, allowing for more heartfelt exchanges. For instance, instead of asking a loved one, "Did you have a good day?" you might ask, "What part of your day meant the most to you?" This invites them to share something significant or reflect on their feelings in a meaningful way, often leading to a more genuine connection.

In professional settings, open-ended questions also set you apart, showing genuine interest and engaging others on a deeper level. Instead of asking, "How long have you been with the company?" you could try, "What do you enjoy most about working here?" This approach prompts thoughtful responses and makes for a more memorable exchange.

Above all, asking thoughtful, open-ended questions can be a catalyst for personal growth. As you seek to understand others' perspectives, you expand your worldview and challenge assumptions. This habit opens the door to new ideas, deeper thinking, and relationships that can enrich your life in surprising ways.

Principle 7: Practice Active Listening

Speaking of listening, this crucial skill lies at the heart of forging meaningful connections. By honing your ability to listen actively, you'll not only deepen your understanding of the other person, but you'll also convey that you truly value their perspective.

Active listening involves far more than just hearing the words someone is saying. It's about being fully present, attuned to verbal and nonverbal cues, and reflecting on what you've heard to ensure accurate comprehension.

Start by maintaining eye contact. This simple gesture communicates that you're focused on the speaker and interested in what they have to say. Avoid the temptation to glance around the room or check your phone - give the other person your undivided attention.

Complement your eye contact with engaged body language. Lean in slightly, nod occasionally, and use open, welcoming gestures. These physical cues let the other person know you're actively listening and processing their words.

Most importantly, resist the urge to interrupt or start formulating your own response while the other person is still speaking. Instead, wait patiently until they've finished, then paraphrase or summarize what you've heard to demonstrate your understanding. You might say something like, "It sounds like you've been dealing with a lot of stress at work lately. Is that accurate?"

By practicing active listening, you communicate respect, empathy, and a genuine desire to understand the other person's perspective. This, in turn, creates an environment of trust and openness - the perfect foundation for forging a meaningful connection.

Principle 8: Find Common Ground

While differences can be fascinating and enriching, the bedrock of any strong interpersonal connection is a sense of shared experience, values, or interests. By taking the time to explore common ground with the people you meet, you open the door to deeper, more rewarding relationships.

Start by paying attention to the small details that emerge organically during your conversation. Do you both have a passion for a certain hobby or sport? Did you grow up in the same region? Do you share a fondness for a particular type of food or music? These seemingly minor similarities can serve as powerful bridges, giving you a natural starting point for further exploration and connection.

As you uncover areas of common ground, don't be afraid to dive deeper. Ask follow-up questions that allow you to learn more about the other person's experiences and perspectives within that shared realm. The more you can find ways to relate to one another, the more comfortable and engaged you'll feel.

Keep in mind that common ground isn't limited to just shared interests and experiences. It can also be found in your core values, beliefs, and aspirations. By listening closely and looking for underlying themes, you may discover that you and the other person have a shared commitment to community service, a deep appreciation for family, or a belief in the power of lifelong learning.

Identifying these deeper points of connection can transform a casual encounter into a meaningful bond. When people sense that you share their fundamental values and priorities, they're far more likely to open up, trust you, and see you as a kindred spirit worthy of their time and attention.

Principle 9: Show Empathy and Understanding

Empathy, the ability to understand and share the feelings of another, is a cornerstone of human interaction. When you demonstrate empathy, you communicate that you value the other person's emotional experience. This validation can be profoundly impactful, especially when meeting someone for the first time. It creates an immediate sense of safety and acceptance, encouraging the other person to open up and engage more deeply.

Understanding goes hand in hand with empathy. It involves making a conscious effort to comprehend the other person's point of view, even if it differs from your own. This willingness to see the world through someone else's eyes is crucial in building connections across diverse backgrounds and experiences.

When you show empathy and understanding, you create a judgment-free zone where people feel comfortable being themselves. This psychological safety is crucial for fostering open, honest communication. It accelerates the trust-building process. When people feel understood, they're more likely to trust you, even in a relatively new relationship.

By showing that you're willing to understand their perspective, you encourage others to share more about themselves, leading to richer, more meaningful exchanges.

In professional or personal contexts, empathy leads to better collaboration. When you understand others' perspectives, you can find solutions that work for everyone. As misunderstandings often arise from a lack of empathy, you can prevent or resolve conflicts more effectively by actively trying to understand others.

People may forget what you said, but they'll remember how you made them feel. Empathy leaves a powerful, positive emotional imprint.

It's important to note that showing empathy doesn't mean you have to agree with everything the other person says or does. It's about acknowledging their right to feelings and experiences, even if they differ from yours.

Principle 10: Being Patient and Present

Being patient and present is fundamental in forging meaningful connections with new people. In our fast-paced world, where distractions are constant and attention spans are dwindling, the ability to slow down and fully engage with others has become increasingly rare and valuable.

Patience allows for the natural unfolding of relationships, giving space for trust to build and genuine understanding to develop. It acknowledges that meaningful connections often take time and can't be rushed.

Being present, on the other hand, involves giving your full attention to the person you're interacting with, setting aside mental distractions, and truly focusing on the moment at hand. This level of engagement communicates respect and genuine interest, making the other person feel valued and heard.

Patience and presence create an environment conducive to deeper conversations and more authentic interactions. They allow you to pick up on subtle cues, both verbal and non-verbal, that might otherwise be missed in a hurried exchange. This attentiveness can lead to more insightful questions and responses, fostering a richer dialogue.

Moreover, when you're patient and present, you're more likely to remember details about the person and your interaction, which can be invaluable for building rapport in future encounters. This principle can set you apart in professional settings, as clients and colleagues appreciate feeling truly listened to and understood.

On a personal level, it can lead to more fulfilling relationships as you create space for genuine connections to flourish. By embodying patience and presence in your interactions with new people, you signal that you value quality over quantity in your relationships, paving the way for deeper, more meaningful connections that can stand the test of time.

Principle 11: Offer a Token of Kindness

Perhaps the most powerful and impactful principle of effective human interaction is the simple act of offering a token of kindness. These unexpected gestures, whether a sincere compliment, an encouraging word, or a small tangible gift, have the ability to transform a chance encounter into a truly memorable experience.

By going beyond the typical social script and investing a piece of yourself in the interaction, you communicate genuine care and concern for the other person. This, in turn, leaves a lasting positive impression and creates the conditions for deeper trust and connection to develop.

The beauty of tokens of kindness is that they come in countless forms, and the impact they have is often outsized compared to the effort required. A heartfelt "That outfit looks great on you!" can brighten someone's day. A few minutes spent listening attentively to their challenges can provide immense comfort. Even a simple gesture like holding the door or offering directions can make a meaningful difference.

The key is to pay attention to the other person and look for authentic opportunities to extend small acts of generosity. What might seem insignificant to you could be exactly what they need to feel seen, valued, and uplifted in that moment. And by making a habit of offering these tokens, you'll find that the ripple effects extend far beyond the initial interaction.

Not only will the recipient of your kindness be positively impacted, but you'll also experience a profound sense of fulfillment and purpose.

As you put these eleven key principles into practice, you'll begin to witness the incredible ripple effects that can emerge from even the most seemingly ordinary interactions. By radiating positive energy, respecting boundaries, engaging with open-ended questions, practicing active listening, finding common ground, and offering tokens of kindness, you have the power to enrich the lives of those you meet and transform your life in profound ways.

One of the most rewarding aspects of this journey is the unexpected ways your actions can create positive change for individuals and within your broader community. Just as Eli's chance encounter with Darryl sparked a movement of compassion and human connection, your own efforts to forge meaningful bonds can have a far-reaching impact.

Perhaps sharing your story of connecting with a stranger will inspire others to follow suit, sparking meaningful discussions and new initiatives aimed at supporting the vulnerable in your community. Or maybe a simple act of kindness you extend to someone in need will be the catalyst that helps them get back on their feet, allowing them to pay that kindness forward to touch the lives of others.

The ripple effects can be astonishing, and the more you embrace the principles of effective human interaction, the more you'll witness these profound transformations unfolding all around you. But the real magic lies in the personal growth and fulfillment you'll experience as you navigate this journey of connection.

As you immerse yourself in the practice of forging genuine bonds with the people you encounter, you'll begin to unlock a deeper understanding of yourself and your place in the world. The lessons you learn, the perspectives you gain, and the connections you build will all contribute to a profound sense of purpose, empathy, and self-awareness.

By embracing the vulnerability required to connect with strangers, you'll find that you're not only making a tangible difference in the lives of others, but you're also nurturing your own emotional and spiritual well-being. The act of truly seeing and being seen by another person has a way of breaking down the walls we often erect to protect ourselves, revealing our shared humanity in powerful and transformative ways.

Moreover, the principles of effective human interaction can serve as a guiding framework for navigating all of your relationships, both personal and professional. As you become more attuned to the subtle cues of those around you, more willing to extend a helping hand or a kind word, and more adept at finding common ground, you'll witness positive impacts in every aspect of your life.

Your colleagues will come to see you as a trusted confidant and collaborative partner. Your friends and family members will feel a deeper sense of connection and understanding. You will develop a heightened sense of emotional intelligence, empathy, and self-awareness - attributes that not only enrich your own life but also position you to become a positive force for change in the lives of those around you.

Ultimately, the true power of the principles of effective human interaction lies in their ability to transform how we approach every new encounter, whether with a complete stranger or a long-time acquaintance. By cultivating this mindset of openness, empathy, and genuine connection, we open ourselves up to the profound and often unexpected ways in which chance meetings can shape our lives and the lives of others.

In a world that can sometimes feel overwhelming and disconnected, the ability to forge these meaningful bonds has never been more vital. By radiating positive energy, respecting personal boundaries, engaging in open-ended dialogue, practicing active listening, finding common ground, and offering tokens of kindness, you have the power to not only uplift and inspire those you meet but also to discover a deeper sense of purpose, empathy, and self-awareness within yourself.

So, embrace the vulnerability, the curiosity, and the sense of adventure that comes with stepping out of your comfort zone and connecting with new people. In doing so, you may find that the most profound and life-changing encounters are the ones that happen by chance - the ones that challenge us, transform us and inspire us to become the best versions of ourselves.

The journey ahead may not always be easy, but it will undoubtedly be rich, rewarding, and full of unexpected discoveries. So, go forth and start forging those meaningful connections, one chance encounter at a time. The world and your own life will be richer for it.

In Affiliation With NCK Organization